THEY LIVED WITH DEATH

Local men in the Battle of Passchendaele 1917.

Fred Holcroft

This edition published by:-

FRED HOLCROFT
Chickamauga.
54, Pemberton Road,
Winstanley,
Wigan
Lancashire
WN3 6DA
Tel:- (01942) 225077

ISBN 0 9524311 3 0

Printed by:-
Douglas Printers Ltd., Woodhouse Drive, Wigan, Lancashire.
Tel:- (01942) 246210

"Only those who have gone over those grim, ghastly, torn and shattered battlefields and lived with death in its entirety can feel the true depth of admiration for the terrible and cruel hardships they had to surmount to take their objective."

Private William Carrington, Park Road, Wigan.
(Wigan Examiner, 17th. October, 1917.)

To

Dennis Martland and Roy Makinson, who have done more than anyone else I know to preserve the memory of those who fell in the Great War, 1914 - 1918.

CONTENTS

MAPS

DIAGRAM

PHOTOGRAPHS

ACKNOWLEDGEMENTS

I would like to thank Frank Taylor who drew the maps, Ian Winstanley who helped prepare the manuscript, Dennis Martland who provided the transcript of his taped interview with Harry Holcroft, John Hannavy and Michael Green for their photographs.

Photographs.
Wigan Heritage Service provided photographs 11, 15, 16, 18 and the front cover from the Manchester Regiment Collection in their Archives.
John Hannavy Collection provided photographs 1, 2, 7, 9, 13 and 17.
Michael Green provided photographs 3, 5, 8 and 10.
The author provided photographs 4, 6, 10, 12, 14 and 19.

Key.
WE = Wigan Examiner.
WO = Wigan Observer.
LJ = Leigh Lournal.

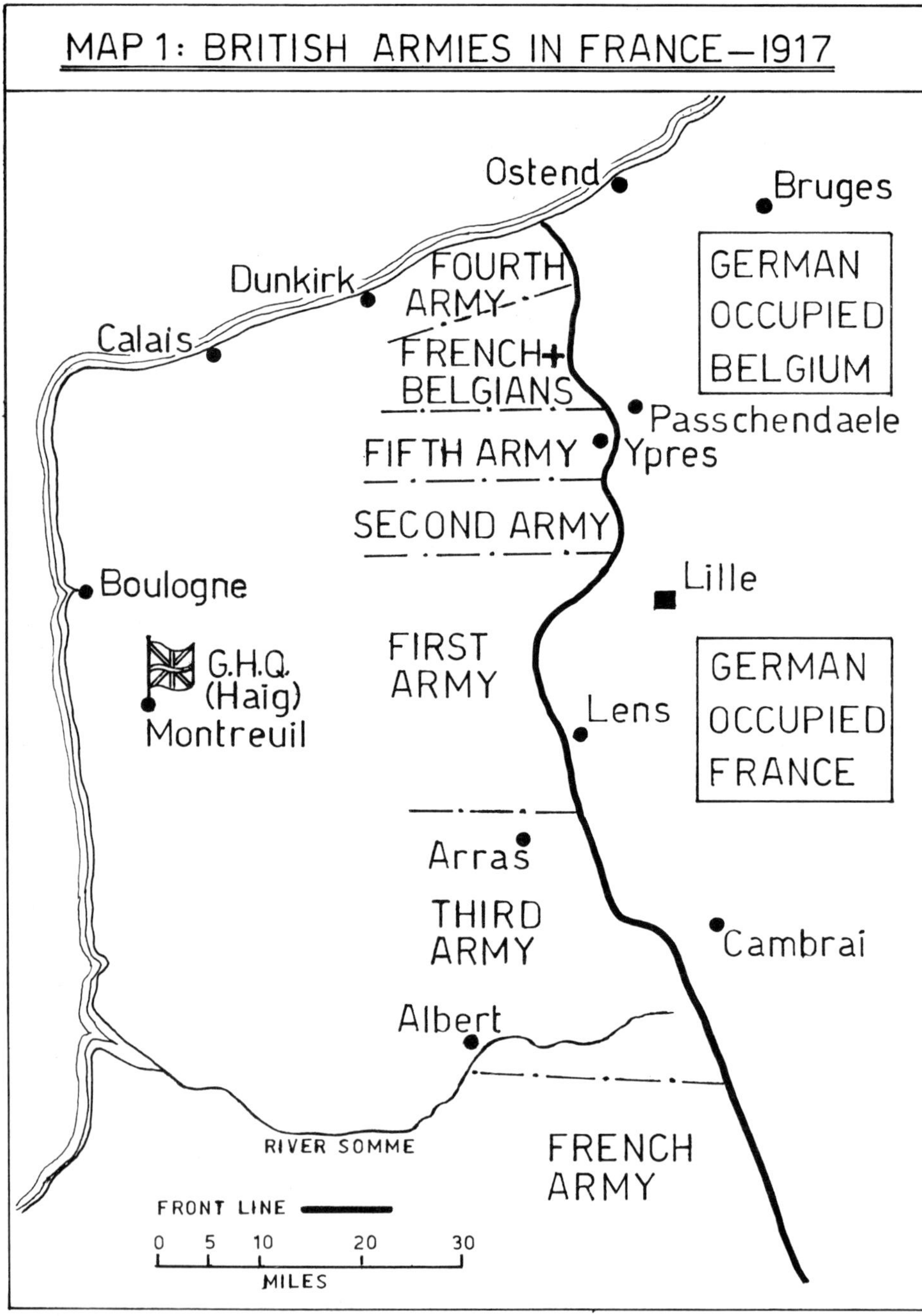
MAP 1: BRITISH ARMIES IN FRANCE—1917
Ostend
Bruges
GERMAN OCCUPIED BELGIUM
Dunkirk
FOURTH ARMY
Calais
FRENCH + BELGIANS
Passchendaele
FIFTH ARMY
Ypres
SECOND ARMY
Boulogne
Lille
G.H.Q. (Haig)
Montreuil
FIRST ARMY
Lens
GERMAN OCCUPIED FRANCE
Arras
THIRD ARMY
Cambrai
Albert
RIVER SOMME
FRENCH ARMY
FRONT LINE
0 5 10 20 30
MILES

INTRODUCTION

In the folklore of military history the name 'Passchendaele' stands for all that is futile in war, slaughter for no gain, purposeless loss of life, muddling through without a definite plan, a completely unnecessary struggle caused by remote senior officers without feelings, divorced from reality and ignorant of the true conditions which the troops in the front line were forced to endure. In November, 1917, after a battle lasting three months and causing over half a million casualties killed, wounded and missing from both sides this hitherto obscure Belgian village was finally taken from the Germans by the Allies. It was not just the size of these losses, terrible as they were, which so sickened both contemporary and subsequent generations, but the awful circumstances under which the battle was fought among scenes of unimaginable, almost indescribable horror as men struggled forward through pouring rain and clinging mud to the accompaniment of thundering crashing high explosive shells, incessantly chattering machine guns and swirling clouds of yellow poisonous gas. This was not all. Of the three million men who were killed on the Western Front during 1914-1918, over 280,000 lie buried in marked or unknown graves in the few square miles around Ypres, casualties of the three battles fought for that town and of the long years of attrition in the trenches of the Ypres Salient. This sacrifice only adds to the mind's - eye view of Passchendaele.

As with many legends, the reality was somewhat different, although in this case not much different. Passchendaele (see Diagram 1) was not a single, continuous battle but several different battles fought at intervals over three months. It was not one long interminable, aimless and merely hopeful thrust but several short, sharp, carefully planned offensives, each with well defined objectives clearly understood by the planners if not by the infantry. Passchendaele should be described as a campaign rather than as a battle. This is not to say that during the time between assaults the infantry were idle. They were kept very busy. Isolated strong points needed taking out, small kinks in the line where the enemy could be a menace to the next attack were straightened, and above all, constant patrolling and probing gave the enemy as little opportunity as possible to strengthen his defences. For the men in the trenches there was no rest.

Weather conditions were not bad throughout the duration of the campaign. Until the really atrocious rainfall began early in October, 1917 there had been very little interference in military operations by the weather. As the campaign reached its climax during the month of

October and victory loomed elusively closer so the weather worsened and the big debate should not be whether or not Passchendaele should ever have been fought at all but whether, once it had been recognised that the conditions had irreversibly worsened, the campaign should have been stopped even if this meant halting only yards short of the ultimate objective on the ground. It all comes down to a reckoning of the price in blood that the British high command was prepared to pay for victory.

And what a price was paid! Fifty-one British and Empire divisions comprising over 150 brigades containing over 600 battalions, a million men, took part at one time or another in the battles around Ypres between 31st. August and 10th. November, 1917. Thousands of local men were involved in the Passchendaele Campaign. This is their story told as far as possible in their own words.

Lest we forget.

CHAPTER ONE - THE YPRES SALIENT.

In August, 1914, faced by war against France and Russia on two fronts, Germany was forced into drastic action. By moving through neutral Belgium, Germany hoped to quickly knock out France and then deal leisurely with Russia. The Germans appreciated that this action would antagonise Great Britain but thought that with the Channel ports in German hands, British intervention would be impossible. It didn't quite work out like that. The Belgians fought back, the British managed to transport their small army across to the Continent and soon two opposing armies were facing each other from two parallel lines of trenches stretching from the Channel to Switzerland.

At first warfare was fluid and was fought in the old style everyone knew. Within a fortnight all available regulars had been transported across the Channel, a tremendous feat of military organisation often overlooked due to the subsequent nature of the war. The Belgians were holding out in their fortifications around Antwerp and Jack Arstall of Preston Road, Standish, was one of the 8,000 strong Royal Naval Division sent to help its defence. After seventeen years in the Royal Navy he had been mobilised from the Reserve on the 15th. July, 1914 and on his return from the front he graphically described what happened to him:-

> "On arriving in Antwerp we were given a rousing reception by the Belgians and any mortal thing we could have, cigars, cigarettes, food, wine anything we liked. The people were so glad to see us that they struggled to touch our hands as we marched past in the street.
>
> We wasted no time in getting into the trenches on the outskirts of the town. There was a fort on our left and another on our right and we were in three lines of trenches between them. The Germans shelled the fort on our left which was about fifty yards from us for sixteen or seventeen hours without a stop using their big guns. We had only our rifles and we had to stand in the trenches and watch the shells bursting. The Germans had the range to a nicety and we watched the shells bursting over it one by one but the fort's guns weren't silenced and we were jumping about trying to dodge the flying pieces of shrapnel. It was like waiting for death. You could hear the big shells buzzing through the air like the noise of a train and whenever one came along somebody would shout *'duck down lads'*. You should have seen the lads dodging out of the way. By gum, I did laugh.

> Our chaps were useless in the trenches as our rifles could not reach the German positions. I only fired eight rounds. Suddenly we got the order to retreat leaving behind everything except our rifles and what was absolutely needed. A quarter of an hour after that the Germans shelled our trenches but they were empty."
> WO 17th. October, 1914.

John Bacon of Garswood was also in the Royal Naval Division at Antwerp:-

> "Ten minutes after I left my trench it was blown away."
> WE 17th. October, 1914.

Allied retreats elsewhere eventually forced the Naval Division to leave the prepared defences around Antwerp, crossing the River Scheldt bridge moments before it was blown up by Belgian engineers in order to delay the German pursuit. As the retreating British crossed the wooden structure they were illuminated by the glare of the adjacent oil tanks owned by the Anglo-American Oil Company set on fire by German shells. The flames shot hundreds of feet into the sky. If the wind had changed direction, they would never have made it.

For over thirty miles they trudged towards the Belgian coast along roads thronged with refugees and blocked with dead horses and abandoned vehicles of all types. Arstall was aghast at what he saw:-

> "We saw some awful sights as we marched back along the roads. Behind us was the city of Antwerp lit up in flames. On the roads were hundreds of people leaving the city and I cried several times at the sight of the suffering I saw. There were women and children, old men and women toiling along with anything on wheels to carry those who could not walk.
> At the end of the march I dropped down for a nod and slept for about half an hour. When I woke up the boys had gone. I came across Lord Curzon who was picking up stragglers. He asked me my battalion. He said, *'you'd better follow me of you want to see England again'*".
> WO 17th. October, 1914.

The bulk of the British army assembled on the Franco-Belgian frontier and boldly advanced northwards into southern Belgium where it hit the advancing German army head-on, in and around the pit headgears and colliery spoil tips of the Belgian coalmining town of

Mons, which must have seemed familiar to the local men, one of whom was Private Joseph Hogan from 71, Lower Morris Street, Wigan.

> "We met the flower of the German army, 200,000 of them and 70,000 of us and I can tell you it was a tidy game until we got the order to retire about four o'clock in the afternoon."
> WO 7th. November, 1914.

The steady accurate rifle fire of the British regulars and reservists mowed down the advancing Germans. So rapid was their rate of fire that the German field officers reported back that the British were using machineguns.

The French divisions which had been ordered to move up from Lorraine to support the British right flank had not arrived. Outnumbered, in danger of being out flanked perhaps even surrounded, the British fell back. Now began the British retreat from Mons. Most units kept in good order but inevitably there was straggling and large numbers of local men were reported missing. Private Hogan again:-

> "There were eight of us cut off from our company and we had a nice three days dodging Uhlan[1] patrols. It was a full fortnight before we found our battalion. They had given us up for lost."
> WO 7th. November, 1914.

The exhausted British regrouped and were reinforced behind the River Marne where they were joined by their French allies. Although Paris seemed at the Germans' mercy, the Allies counterattacked and drove the invaders back. Now it was the Germans' turn to retreat and they were soon leaving behind a trail of dead and wounded soldiers, dead horses and looted houses. On the River Aisne, the Germans turned to stand and once more the fighting intensified. Cavalry were still involved at this stage and Private Leyland from Spring Street of the 4th. Dragoon Guards had three horses shot from under him. Private Thomas Alker of 181, Warrington Road, Goose Green in the 17th. Lancers patrolled the flanks to stop the German cavalry raids and while he was carrying a message across country his horse was killed by a shell but he luckily escaped with just bruising. A former regular, he had been called up from the Reserve while serving in the Wigan Borough police.

[1] German cavalry, usually lancers.

Another Wigan policeman now in khaki was P.C. Scott whose former beat had included Hardybutts. He wrote home:-

> "I have had some exciting times and I can honestly assure you that at times it has been a bit more lively than Scholes.'
> WO 21st. November, 1914.

Both sides began to dig in and the fighting increased in tempo still further. Herbert Carrington wrote home to Wigan from his hospital bed:-

> "I was put on outpost with two others. We were fifty or sixty yards in front of our firing line. We laid down and made ourselves as comfortable as possible. I had not been laid down many minutes when I spotted a German, he was driving stakes in the ground for fastening barbed wire on. Well I loaded my rifle and took steady aim. I don't know whether I killed him or not but anyway he dropped and never moved again.'
> WO 1st. December, 1914.

Field artillery was used more and more. A single shell dropped near Carrington and killed twelve men and five horses. Driver J. Hitchen of the Royal Field Artillery wrote to a neighbour in Newtown, Wigan:-

> "Seven days under shellfire night and day. Our first casualty was (sic) a corporal and a sergeant. A big shell struck one of the guns and smashed it to scrap. While all the gunners were blown to bits. Then we lost that Wigan chap I told you about and forty six horses as well as our major and lieutenant.'
> WE 14th. November, 1914

Ernest Cherrington from Cambridge Street, Wigan was also in the artillery. The war was not yet three months old and already ninety nine men out of one hundred and nineteen in his battery were casualties and of the two hundred original horses brought from England none were left. Prophetically he wrote:-

> "You can tell those people who think that the war will be over by Christmas that they are quite mistaken."
> WE 28th. November, 1914.

MAP 2: THE YPRES SALIENT—1917

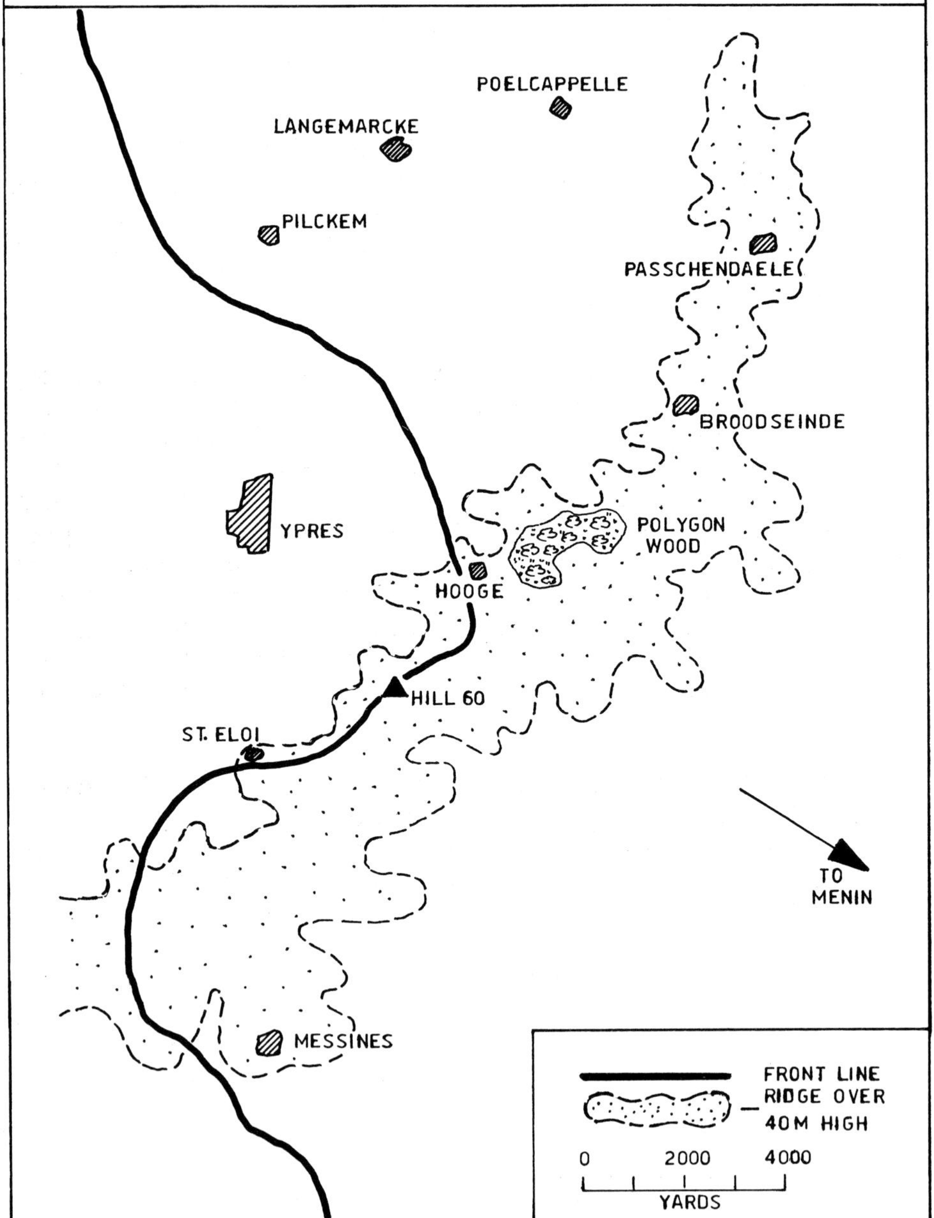

As the first winter of the war closed in there were ominous references in letters home alluding to heavy rainfall, water-filled trenches and the cloying effects of mud.

Both sides had tried to take the vital Belgian rail junction of Ypres and the British had won. Sergeant Andrew Joyce from Standish of the Royal Munster Fusiliers reported:-

> "When we walked into Ypres it was one of the loveliest places in the world. The Germans were under the impression that the place was theirs and when they found out that they were wrong they shelled the beautiful buildings, razed them to the ground and made it a heap of ruins. It was deliberate destruction."
> WE 14th. January, 1915.

So the Ypres Salient was born. A salient is a wedge of territory extending into the enemy's position and so is exposed to attack from three sides. Although the British army had saved Ypres, the Germans had almost surrounded them (see Map 2) and the Ypres Salient became extremely difficult to hold. Worse still, the British-held territory was a low lying triangle of land completely overlooked by the higher German-held ground to the east which gave the enemy a perfect view of everything that moved on the British side. For three years trench warfare raged and death came in many forms. In a charge to capture the German trenches opposite, death seemed inevitable. Private James Welsby of the 2/Lancashire Fusiliers was a lucky survivor of a night attack:-

> "My platoon advanced in support of the Argyll and Sutherland Highlanders. Twenty-one of us went out and the enemy opened up with maxims and rifles. In the dark the flashes resembled floodlights in the theatre. Only nine of us came back."
> WE 27th. February, 1915.

Sergeant Joyce was a tough Irishman but:-

> "I don't want to see a bayonet charge any more. I saw them shot down on my right and my left and every moment not knowing but it might be my last."
> WE 14th. January, 1915.

Shelling by German artillery, on the front-line firing trenches, rest dugouts and on rear areas, was at the same time ever present and haphazard. It concentrated on a particular target yet no one knew where an individual shell might fall. A man could be blown to fragments or escape unscathed. Most feared were the big German shells which caused lots of black smoke the men called 'Jack Johnsons' after the American negro boxer with a big knockout punch. It made a hole twelve feet deep and thirty feet wide:-

> "When it bursts a quarter of a mile away it gives you a good shaking. If it strikes anyone you need a brush to sweep up the pieces."
> WE 23rd. January, 1915.

Private Percival of the 8th.(Irish) King's Liverpool Regiment, son of Wigan's Chief Constable used a local nickname for the big shells:-

> "The 'coal boxes' make a wail like a back-wall cat and shake the earth when they go off but shrapnel can't be heard coming. All you hear is zip-bang and the pieces are like the noise of a bee around you."
> WO 15th. June, 1915.

These smaller shells containing shrapnel fragments were just as dangerous. They burst in the air above the trenches and showered sharp debris on the troops below. Private Webb again:-

> "Jones, the man next to me was struck with shrapnel when he was looking up and his head and two arms were blown away."
> WE 27th. February, 1915.

No one was immune from the shelling. Private J. Hodgson, formerly chauffeur to Mr. Edmundson of Garswood Hall Collieries, drove a wagon carrying ammunition to the artillery batteries, running the gauntlet of German 17lb. shells for six or seven miles. One hit would have finished him.

The German stick grenade was a deadly missile, yet early on their war machine had to rely home-made 'bombs':-

> "Five jam pot bombs landed on the roof of our dugout and exploded but hurt no one. They are made of old jam tins and

explode eight or ten seconds after touching the ground. You have just got time to pick them up and throw them away."
WE 13th. March, 1915.

Snipers were a constant menace at all times. The man next to Corporal Page from Golborne had his hair parted by a bullet and as the sergeant raised himself to full height shouting a reprimand, he was shot through the forehead. Every movement in the trenches had to be concealed.

Private John Butterworth from Horwich, a territorial in the Loyal North Lancashires described one of the routines the men had to perform:-

> "I did two hours at the listening post. This is a kind of dugout thirty yards in front of our trenches. It is quite exciting (sic) as you imagine you hear all kinds of sounds, even footsteps coming towards you. You can hear the Germans singing and talking even though they are five hundred yards away."
> WE 6th. April, 1915.

During the day the men stood guard for an hour and then stood down for five, while at night the ratio was one hour on but only two off.

The local home front was not a safe haven either. The coal mines that the volunteers left behind were dangerous workplaces and so was the Roburite Works at Gathurst where the ammonal used in underground mines was made. On Monday 15th. May, 1916 there was an explosion which could be heard for miles and when the smoke and dust cleared, seven men were dead and twenty four injured. An inquest was held immediately but due to wartime censorship its findings were not published in the local papers until after the war ended. One witness interviewed by the Coroner was William Gore:-

> "The foreman Alfred Evans[1] and me were the only two in the place when the fire broke out in one of the pans in which the explosive was being made. The pan had been charged an hour before. I heard a hissing sound and found one mixer was in flames. I stopped the machine and got an extinguisher which I played on the fire for about five minutes until the extinguisher was done. Then I went into one of the other sheds for some more

[1] He died from his injuries next day.

extinguishers and when I got back the whole place was in flames and the men were playing on the fire with hose pipes."

Thomas Cooksey the assistant manager continued with further evidence:-

"The smoke changed from a khaki yellow to an intense blue-black and I said to the men, *'clear out you fellows for God's sake, run jump and drop.'* The men had run about fifteen to twenty yards when the explosion occurred and they were caught in the open."

There were four small explosions then a large one and the debris was scattered for two hundred yards. During the twenty-nine year history of the factory which had made explosives for the local coal mines, there had never been an explosion. Foreign matter in the charcoal, probably flint nodules, started the fire but the giant explosion was caused by the explosive which had already been manufactured being stored in the machine-shed because the storage magazine was full!

Back on the Western Front the geological conditions of the Ypres Salient were typical of western Flanders, an extremely flat low lying plain everywhere only a few feet above sea level. There were no hills, merely gentle slopes leading up to round knolls or long ridges graced with the name 'hill' and usually named after their height. The famous 'Hill 60' was so called because it was sixty metres (195 feet) above sea level yet it was over twenty miles inland! This lack of height and slope was fatally combined with the high level of the underground water table where the top of the water reservoir in the porous chalk rock was usually just a few feet beneath the surface of the ground, sometimes even soaking up into the superficial surface deposits of clay and sand which covered the solid bedrock. Over the centuries the poor natural drainage had been improved through land reclamation schemes so that an intricate pattern of ditches and canals had evolved but this delicate system only needed slightly disturbing through heavy rain or neglect to be turned into a waterlogged morass. A combination of both was disastrous. Three years of warfare, particularly from the heavy shelling, had wreaked havoc with the natural drainage of the salient which added discomfort to the hazardous nature of trench warfare.

These conditions, which were to dominate the fighting on the Western Front for four years came as an unexpected shock. Private Davies from Wigan found himself in a trench full of water:-

"We thought that after bailing the water out we could make the trench deeper, but imagine our feelings when after emptying it, when we inserted a spade in the floor and it filled up again."
WO 31st. July, 1915.

A Wiganer in the Grenadier Guards wrote home to describe life in the trenches:-

"The day time passes quickly but the nights drag. Pitch dark, occasionally starlight, rockets sent up by both sides to see that all is clear, a few shots perhaps a machine gun sweeping the parapets, and the big guns now and then sending souvenirs across. That is the order which is monotonous although it gets lively at times. The country is flooded so you can guess what the trenches are like."
WO 1st. January, 1916.

As early as the first winter of the war the Flanders mud was influencing events in the front line. Lieutenant Barry Swales in peacetime a shop assistant in his father's King Street jewellers' shop wrote home:-

"I never knew there could be so much mud as this. When you are making your way to a trench, each foot feels as if you have a 56lb. weight on it."
WE 20th. March, 1915.

Corporal Prudence from Boar's Head, Standish, described carrying ammunition up to the front at night:-

"... over fields of mud up to our necks (sic) and over streams and small trenches and shell holes full of water. It was pitch dark and I could not see a foot in front of me. I fell a dozen times."
WO 2nd. March, 1915.

Used to plenty of water working down the pit before the war, Private Harry Holcroft (no relation) from Crawford village was shocked by conditions in the trenches:-

"It was a terrible place. The trenches was full of water. We was bailing water out of the trenches all the time all night over. Wc

> had to wear waders in the traverses and trenches. We had to walk on duck boards to get to the front line. The farmers' drains were bursted everywhere and we were waterlogged."

Sheltering from the rain under a tarpaulin, warmed only by a wood fire which gave off suffocating fumes and choking smoke, Holcroft was put out of action with a wheezy chest.

For the moment the most obvious changes were the destruction caused, it must be said, by both sides. Constable Beattie, a Wigan policeman on military service in Belgium, wrote home to his former colleagues:-

> "There is a tremendous amount of damage to property. The villages which used to be here are quite literally blown to pieces and live shells have gone through even into the cellars. It is surprising the amount of bird life here, birds singing in the trees and swallows building nests in the ruins while the guns roar."
> WO 4th. July, 1817.

For the troops these unusual ground conditions, found nowhere else on the Western Front outside Flanders, meant that it was impossible for the British soldiers to dig normal trenches as they subsequently filled with water. There were no comfortable underground dugouts in which to shelter from the elements and from German shelling. By contrast the Germans, usually on the defensive, built concrete bunkers above ground and camouflaged them with turf sods. When these dried out they were blasted off the bunkers' roofs by the explosions of the British artillery shells exposing the white concrete. From a distance they looked like small round pill-boxes and were so named. These defensive strong points, though small in size were immensely powerful and the British were only able to examine them closely after their capture. Following the attack on Bottle Wood near Messines, one local soldier examined the captured pill-boxes and wrote home incredulously:-

> "Some of his concrete dugouts hadn't been damaged much by the artillery bombardment and no wonder for they were five of six feet thick with machine gun emplacements and a hole at the top for a periscope. He had been pretty secure in them these two and half years!"
> LJ 13th. July, 1917.

Another local soldier equally impressed wrote:-

> "It is a sight to see what preparations they had made during the years they had been in occupation of it (the Messines Ridge) ... concrete roofs where in their opinion no shell could penetrate."
> WO 4th. July, 1917.

These artificial constructions were yet another handicap in addition to the wretched conditions underfoot during the forthcoming British advances of 1917. Throughout 1916, British efforts had been diverted elsewhere, notably to the big Somme offensive further south and the Ypres sector was relatively quiet, but in the spring of 1917 all eyes turned one more to the Ypres Salient.

CHAPTER TWO - WHY PASSCHENDAELE?

Why was the Ypres sector chosen for the big offensive of 1917? True there were acute tactical needs. The small salient everywhere overlooked by the Germans occupying the higher ground to the east desperately needed to be enlarged by pushing the enemy back off the ridges so that the British rear echelons could be unobserved by German spotters and out of artillery range. German occupation of the slopes to the east gave them immense advantages. Constable Beattie continues:-

> "The Germans were started on the ridge, something like looking down Wigan Lane into Standishgate. Our boys were below and there was scarcely a piece of ground that had not been searched by the German artillery."
> WO 4th. July, 1917.

In addition to the dire tactical situation, there were important strategic considerations. At all costs the Germans had to be diverted from the French sector of the Western Front. In April, 1917, General Nivelle's offensive on the River Aisne had failed with huge losses of manpower. Disheartened by years of failure and stalemate, French civilian morale had plummeted. Worse still, deterioration in army morale on a large scale had made several French divisions incapable defending themselves if attacked! Beginning with a number of individual desertions, discontent in the ranks rapidly spread to refusals to obey orders, demonstrations against the war, and activities by organised agitators culminating in outright mutiny, quaintly termed in the records as 'acts of collective indiscipline'.

At sea, the German U-boats were increasingly successful, sinking two million tons of shipping in the first six months of 1917, so that their bases along the Belgian coastline currently in German hands were a danger that had to be eliminated. There were even fanciful suggestions that a successful offensive would clear the Germans out of Belgium altogether.

On the Eastern Front the rapidly deteriorating military situation meant that Russia might make a separate peace treaty so enabling Germany to transfer fifty divisions to the West. An Allied offensive would sap German strength and prevent a German attack until 1918 when the American troops were due to arrive. The U.S.A. had entered the war on the 6th. April, 1917 but were not able to put an army into the field immediately.

MAP 3: PLANNED OFFENSIVE—1917

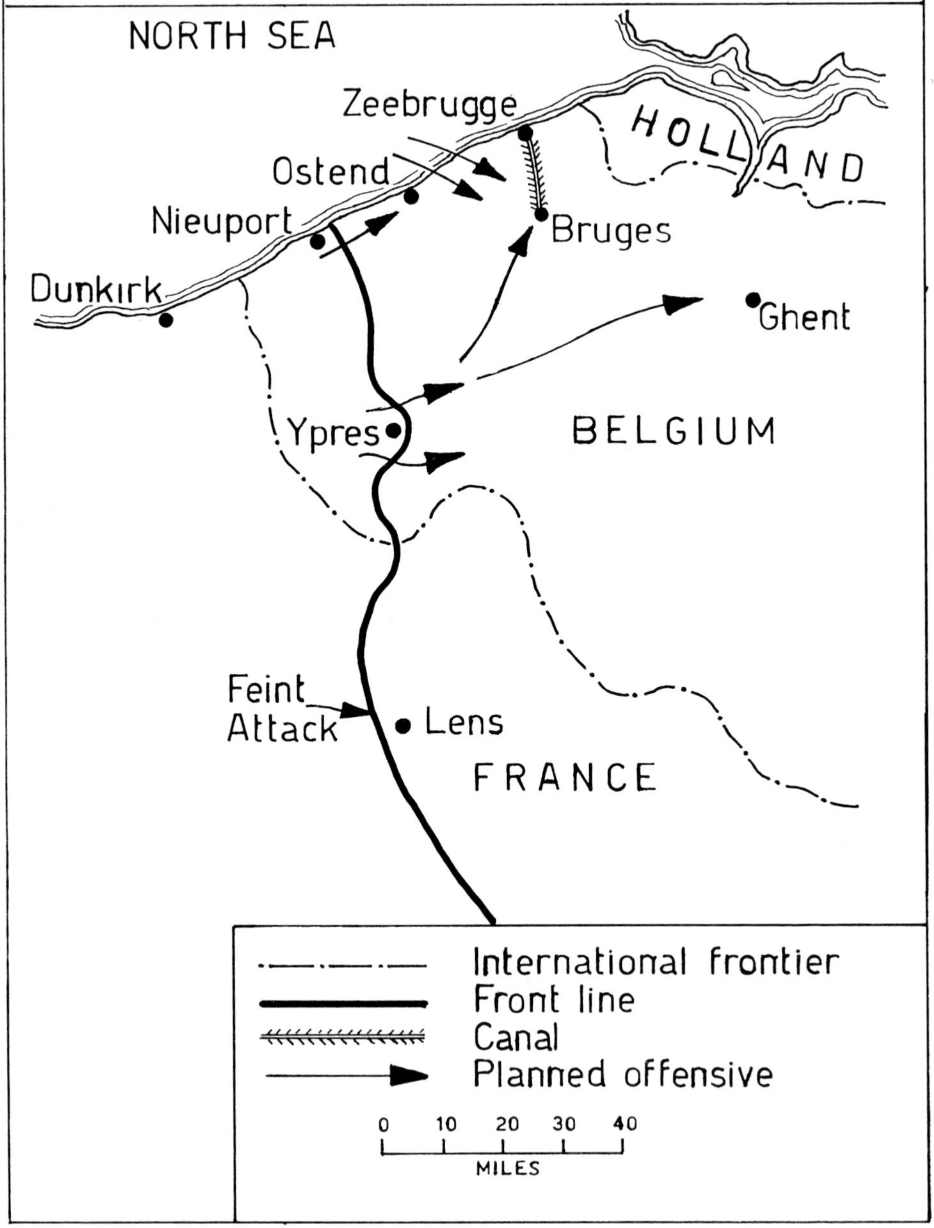

The Allies were greatly encouraged by their intelligence reports. German manpower reserves were approaching exhaustion, already in 1917 the classes of 1918, 1919 and 1920 were being called up. Rations and equipment for the front-line troops were being reduced and the effects of the Allied blockade on Germany was causing severe shortages on the home front especially in fuel and food. Statements by captured prisoners and letters from home in their possession showed that both military and civilian morale was collapsing. An offensive was essential in order to take advantage of this and only the British were capable of making it.

On the British home front there were stirrings of discontent and throughout 1917, pressure for peace grew. That year the Socialist International held the Stockholm Peace Conference in neutral Sweden and the British Labour Party indeed the labour movement as a whole, were deeply divided as to the conference's motives and usefulness. The local soldiers mostly from the working classes were intensely interested in both. All the letters published in the local press portrayed the peace movement as a betrayal of the fighting men:-

> "Make them (the pacifists) cross the battlefields of Flanders. They would get peace all right but it would be like the crosses our boys get over the places they fall. R.I.P. Ripped In Pieces. If they make anything out of their peace move I will think I have wasted a valuable three years of my life with nothing to show for it. Of course everybody wants peace but it must be the one we want. When the war came we were not prepared and now after three years of sufferings and privations we are not going to have any kind of peace."
> WO 1st. September, 1917.

And:-

> "All pacifists are not bribed with German gold, the real matter with the average pacifist is not treachery but soft headedness and a childish willingness to believe the bare words of self-confessed scoundrels who treat international contracts as pie-crusts, who murder for glory and whose cardinal virtue of faith is that the end justifies the means."
> WO 8th. January, 1918.

Stephen Walsh, the Ince Labour M.P., threw himself whole heartedly behind the war effort and had no time for pacifists:-

> "We must do nothing which would give comfort to the enemy. I can imagine nothing more infamous than the conduct of those who have gone out of their way month after month making misrepresentations and bringing obloquy on their own country."
> WO 11th. August, 1917.

When the conference of British socialists voted to attend the Stockholm meeting, Walsh advocated the withholding of the delegates passports by the British Government. His local political ally, Harry Twist, the Wigan miners' leader held similar views:-

> "It is the supreme duty of the people of this country to fill up the ranks and pile up the munitions, refuse no sacrifice to help those brave lads at the front."
> WO 13th. February, 1917.

Yet during 1917 a negotiated peace giving Germany most of her war aims seemed a real possibility. The war had already lasted three years with no end in sight. War-weariness was beginning to stir in even the previously enthusiastic. Cynicism was everywhere. The country had made great efforts in men, money and material, with huge losses and with very little to show for it. By this time even from a small area like Leigh and district over 5,000 men were serving in the armed forces, and already 370 had been killed, yet the war went on. It was against this background that future military operations had to be planned.

Above everything else stood the towering presence of the British Army Commander-in-Chief, Sir Douglas Haig. He believed in the value of the offensive and that the British Army unaided by its French allies, was capable not only of a break through in Flanders but also of pushing the Germans out of Belgium altogether. His determination, nay obstinacy, drove the offensive onwards when others were calling for a halt. He believed that if he was to break the enemy army it could only be done in Flanders where there was no space in the German rear for a strategic withdrawal to a better prepared position as the Germans had done in 1916 after their battering on the Somme.

Given the tactical and strategical situation in 1917, Flanders was the only sector where an offensive could be made. Whether or not it stood any chance of success was an entirely different matter.

CHAPTER THREE - PROLOGUE.

Messines Ridge, 7th. - 14th. June, 1917.

The first task of the British offensive was to capture the ridge to the south of Ypres held by the Germans since the start of the war which would give a solid base for the main British strike towards the north. As events turned out the Battle of Messines Ridge turned out to be the British Army's greatest victory of the First World War. It was a brilliant offensive combination of infantry, artillery and engineers which gained all its objectives. Along a frontage of 167,000 yards, three attacking corps, IX Corps, X Corps and II ANZAC Corps, each deployed three divisions in line. Three more divisions were in reserve and the attack was supported by a strong concentration of artillery and by the explosion of nineteen mines which had been secretly in place beneath the German lines for some time.

Months before, starting in the spring of 1915, a series of underground tunnels had been dug in this sector. Starting in the rear of the British trenches, they had been driven in varying lengths from 800 to 2,000 yards ending some 80 to 90 feet directly beneath the German front line. Machinery constantly broke down and the bulk of the work was done by hand. Many local soldiers were former coal miners and had been drafted into the tunnelling teams where they worked in gangs of eight with four digging and shoring the tunnel and the other four filling sandbags with the extracted material. It was slow work, even for the experienced colliers and only 30-40 sandbags were produced per shift. Four days' digging were followed by four days' rest. Natural conditions were awful in the waterlogged strata and there was always the danger of being blown up by German counter-mining but the pay was good, 6/- (30p) per day compared with 1/- (5p) per day for the infantry in the trenches.

The Flanders soil was of crucial importance. The upper layer of yellow sand, constantly blasted by artillery, lay on top of the blue clay in which the tunnels were dug. Great care had to be taken to hide the material extracted so that its tell-tale colouring would not betray the digging to the enemy. Conditions underground could not have been more different from those in the coal mines back home. The loose clay and sand was unlike the solid rock strata which protected the coal seams, and was so waterlogged that it was like digging through quicksand. Only with the greatest difficulty were the roof and sides shored up with boards.

Many local men employed on this work, like Sapper John O'Neil from Leigh, wrote home giving descriptions of their activities but for security reasons their letters were censored and a valuable source of information on an important sphere of activity was lost. Not even the 'Daily Mail' correspondent, Valentine Williams, gave away many military secrets in a report reprinted locally:-

> "I went down a mine the other night, down a shaft supported by baulks of timber resembling a street manhole, a greasy knotted rope the means of descent and candles stuck to the baulks with their own grease providing the illumination. At the foot of the shaft stood a cheerful person smothered from head to foot in yellow clay and a second man emerged from the entrance of a low gallery which ran at right angles from the shaft bottom. He was a thickset, well-developed man similarly dressed in sleeveless singlet and trousers tucked into trench boots and similarly daubed with yellow clay, even in his hair and round his eyes. The two of them carried on a conversation regarding the perverse inclination of the clay to stick to them. When I asked them where they came from one replied, "Frum Wiggin", and disappeared off down the gallery. I followed him. Imagine a low earth tunnel running as straight as a die through the clay and despite a plank floor, ankle deep in mud and water, with chill damp air and water dripping continually from the roof. At the end of the tunnel was a third man also, "Frum Wiggin" as it turned out, hacking away at the wall of clay in front of him with a pick and shovel. Tallow candles cast a feeble light."
> WO 1st. June, 1915.

The Germans counter-attacked both below ground where their counter-mining tunnels broke into the British workings and subterranean fights began and and above ground by night-time raids across No-Man's-Land. One night, Lance-corporal George Paddock, Royal Engineers, of 3, Alfred Street, Tyldesley, found himself alone guarding a mine shaft entrance during a German trench raid. He fought them off single handedly and saved the lives of the men below ground, being awarded the Military Medal.

Only when hostilities ended did the full story emerge of the part played by local men in the British army's tunnelling activities, when William Lowe, a mining engineer with the Pearson and Knowles Coal and Iron Company and a former lieutenant in the Royal Engineers, addressed a meeting of the Past and Present Students' Association of Wigan and District Mining and Technical College on the subject of,

MAP 4 : THE MINES AT MESSINES — 7 June 1917

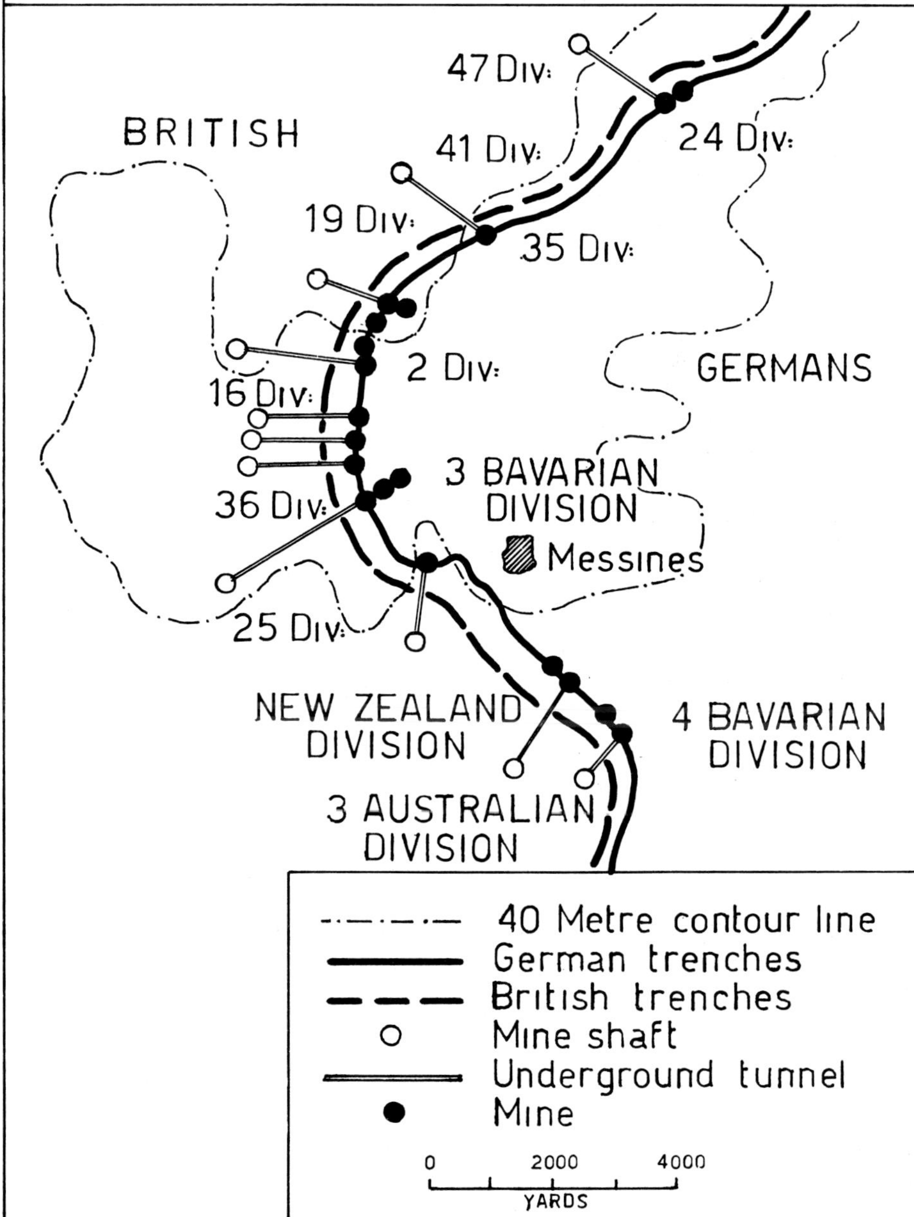

'Tunnelling in France. Illustrated with chalk drawings on the blackboard.' (WO 22nd. November, 1919.)

> "The infantry commanders were told to ask for volunteers to work underground and as one man the miners came forward. Unfortunately the infantry commanders took the chance to get rid of their undesirable characters as well! Still, by June, 1916, there were about 25,000 men engaged in mining and by April, 1917 almost all the line was protected by mines[1] and counter-mines."

The first batch of tunnellers, all former coal miners and strong trade unionists, lined up before a staff officer and listened to a pep talk on how vital was this new work, shuffling uneasily on hearing that the tunnellers would get six shillings a shift while the assistants would get two shillings and tuppence! On the conclusion of the talk, the staff officer barked. *'Assistants step forward!'* Not a man moved. Perplexed, the officer shouted, *'Tunnellers step forward!'* All the men took one pace to the front. The officer shook his head. *'You can't all be tunnellers, we must have some assistants.'* The voice of an ex-miner came out of the ranks to put the officer straight, *'Its owl reight mester, them two 'un tuppence men is awl cummin termorrer.'* They all got the same rate! Lowe continued:-

> "The 253rd. Tunnelling Company, Royal Engineers in which I first served commenced operations in December, 1915. We sank and connected eight shafts covering a distance of about three miles. These shafts were four feet by six feet and twenty yards deep in hard blue clay."

Lowe explained the security aspects:-

> "When working in clay and sand absolute silence was essential. In the galleries conversation was prohibited and no one was allowed to walk around unnecessarily and when work was in progress one could scarcely hear anything but the heavy breathing of the men. Listening saved your life and we soon got to know not to work when the Boche was quiet (because they were listening) but that it was safe when they were making a noise.

[1] Tunnels.

At first the listening was done by the naked ear but this method was far too uncertain. Then we had an instrument sent to us after the method of a doctor's stethoscope but instead of the little horn there was a sound box fitted. After a little practice you could tell what the enemy was doing within a distance of one hundred feet in chalk or ten to twelve feet in clay. After this the geophone was invented, similar to the previous one but with two sound boxes and in chalk picking could be heard up to two hundred and fifty feet and at one hundred feet all of the enemy's movements could be heard and recorded. After that came the electric listening system were two men at the pit bottom could listen to twenty or thirty places. This was a big improvement because before that we had to have one man in every place and if the Boche blew his mine that man was caught.

At first the clay was cut by means of a push-pick but this was too slow, only three or four feet of progress made per twelve hour shift. It was the we started clay-picking[1] and doubled our progress. We holed about eighteen inches deep with a push-pick then we fixed up a wooden frame for the picker to lie on and the cut from the floor to the roof was taken off with a grafting tool. Believe me, clay picking was hard work, twelve hours on and thirty six hours off.

The ventilation was done by either a huge pair of bellows or a Holman air pump. When the ventilator was three hundred feet from the point to be ventilated, there wasn't what the Coal Mines Act would call an 'adequate amount' of air (laughter from audience). When working near the old blows there was that most deadly of gases, carbon monoxide. The gas, as you know, is given off in huge volumes when explosives are used. It lay in pockets in the chalk and was often given off in puffs sometimes after a blow. This necessitated our working with canaries and when the canary dropped off the perch, the men came out (more laughter). In other places we used two connecting shafts hoping the draft would work and the candle would not blow out (yet more laughter).

We moved to Girvenchy where we found things in a very bad state. Owing to enormous quantities of water, the galleries were only ten or twelve feet deep. We had to clear out every time our own fellows set off their trench mortars!

[1] The local reporter must have mis-heard the term 'clay-kicking.'

In this area the Boche had us beaten. Whenever and wherever we ran a sap he was waiting. In one week he wrecked our galleries three times. After this we decided that in spite of the water we would go deeper and consequently we got a shaft down to thirty feet deep, nine feet by four feet six inches and divided into two compartments, one for winding and one for pumping. In order to keep the mines dry we had twenty men working pumps and with eight hour shifts we needed sixty men for pumping alone. But it was no use. Whatever we tried failed.

We then moved to Callone where one day we had a shock We were pushing out one day when our sapper had the shock of his life. He hit the face with his pick, the chalk fell out and there in front of him was a tin box. He made the hole large and saw more tin boxes. He had struck a German mine ready charged to fire. He dropped his tools and left the gallery, taking his men with him. The officer commanding was sent for and two officers went down, one with a flashlight, the other with his revolver drawn. About four yards from the charge the flashlight shone on it and on seeing the reflection, thinking he saw something move, the officer with the revolver fired into it! Nothing happened but both officers cleared out pretty quickly.

A council of war was held at the pit top and it was decided to call for volunteers to go down the shaft and remove the charge. One officer, an N.C.O. and six men went down into the gallery when the Boche blew his mine, about 1,500lbs. of Perdite which gives off lots of smoke. This came along our gallery, up the shaft and when the Boche put up a Very light it (the smoke) showed up like a house on fire. Then he started with his flying pigs and trench mortars etc. He knocked the shaft in and completely levelled the trenches. As well as the casualties below two officers and four men were killed.

Shortly after we heard the enemy approaching us in our other shaft so we started two inclined shafts away to the right. When he got within twenty feet of our shaft we very slowly and quietly charged up (laid the explosive) and tamped (sealed the explosive with bagged chalk). We waited two days until he started working then we blew. We then went out to the left until we were about forty feet ahead of our old gallery, heard the Boche working again, stopped, waited to let him get within ten feet of us then blew him again. Then off we went again, heard him a third time and blew him again. We had reached within twenty feet of his front line so we decided to sit tight there.

In another shaft we heard the enemy on our left and waited. He seemed to be running parallel to us. We blew and immediately started to work towards him. We broke through to his gallery and found four of the enemy dead. We went on and kept hearing noises but from where? Then we realised that to beat us the Boche had gone even deeper. We ran an incline down eighty feet dipping one in two. Here we struck laterals left and right and ran out listening posts. At this depth the chalk was so hard it was impossible to cut it with a pick so we got some drilling machines and explosives and blasted our way along. Working in chalk, noise does not matter but speed does. We ran out a listening post one hundred and twelve feet in sixty four hours, the fastest work we ever did. Needless to say there was no Coal Mines Act (laughter) or we should not have got along so quickly.
The listener using the electric listening apparatus at the pit bottom reported noises at post No. 8. The officer commanding, Captain Dickson and I went down and were able to place his direction, which if he kept on would take him just past No.8. When he got close I wanted to blow but Captain Dickson said, *'No we'll let him pass then blow.'* He got so close we could hear him walking about. This is where the electric listener saved my life. At the start of one shift, I went to the pit bottom and the listener reported no movement for four hours. *'Right,'* said Captain Dickson, *'We'll just sit and wait a while.'* We sat down and discussed the previous day's football match between the tunnelling officers and the army officers. The Captain was just saying the centre ought to have passed to the wing when up went No.8! We all made a dash for the ladder! Fortunately no one was lost but when we inspected later No.8 was closed up as if it had never existed while the lateral was reduced from four feet to one foot six inches. If it had not been for the electric apparatus we would have been in No.8 trying to find out what the Boche was doing."

As Spring 1917 arrived, after six weeks of frost the weather improved and the time for the attack drew nearer. Morale rose in the British ranks and following an awful winter of illness, frostbite and trenchfoot, the troops were rareing to go. Corporal T. Platt of Tyldesley wrote:-

"It has been a hard time for the men but we have come out of it well and these last few days of sunshine have raised our spirits."
LJ 6th. March, 1917.

Throughout May, 1917, a huge concentration of artillery was assembled south of Ypres until a total of 2,266 guns and howitzers were in place giving a three to one superiority over the Germans. During the preliminary bombardment from 26th. May until 6th. June, 1917, over three and half million shells were fired (29 shells per yard of front) over twice the amount fired at the Somme in 1916.

During the evening of the 6th-7th June, 1917, the troops gathered, bayonets fixed, in their assembly trenches. Lieutenant Henry Buckmaster, an old boy of Rossall School and the son of the vicar of Hindley, wrote of his feelings:-

> "We marched off quietly, hardly a sound being made save the dull sound of our footsteps on the soft ground. Everybody seemed to recognise the solemnity of the occasion and scarcely a whisper was uttered. We passed through cultivated fields and everything presented such a strange contrast to war. It seemed impossible to conceive that we were going into battle. We marched on steadily until we came to the places which had been rendered desolate by shell fire and we heard more shells coming over. These only made a slight explosion and we soon found out the reason why. There was a curious smell and someone shouted, "Gas!" We put on our (gas) helmets and were able to breathe freely but the perspiration from our faces soon dimmed the glasses and rendered it difficult to see our way. In a short time we were able to take our helmets off. This happened half a dozen times on our march."

At ten past three in the morning, the mines, each containing 48,000lbs (21 tons) of ammonal explosive, were exploded at twenty one-second intervals. Altogether one million pounds of ammonal was exploded. Half a pound would have been enough to destroy Wigan Town Hall. The effect was devastating.

> "Nineteen enormous mushrooms rose up slowly and majestically out of the ground then split into pieces with a mighty roar sending up multi-coloured columns of flame mixed with earth and splinters high up into the sky."
> Von Kuhl: Der Weltkrieg 1914-18. p.453.

A watching British officer wrote to his local paper:-

> "Yesterday, starting at 3.15 a.m., we blew two (sic) mines up under Fritz. The shock was enough to knock one off one's feet

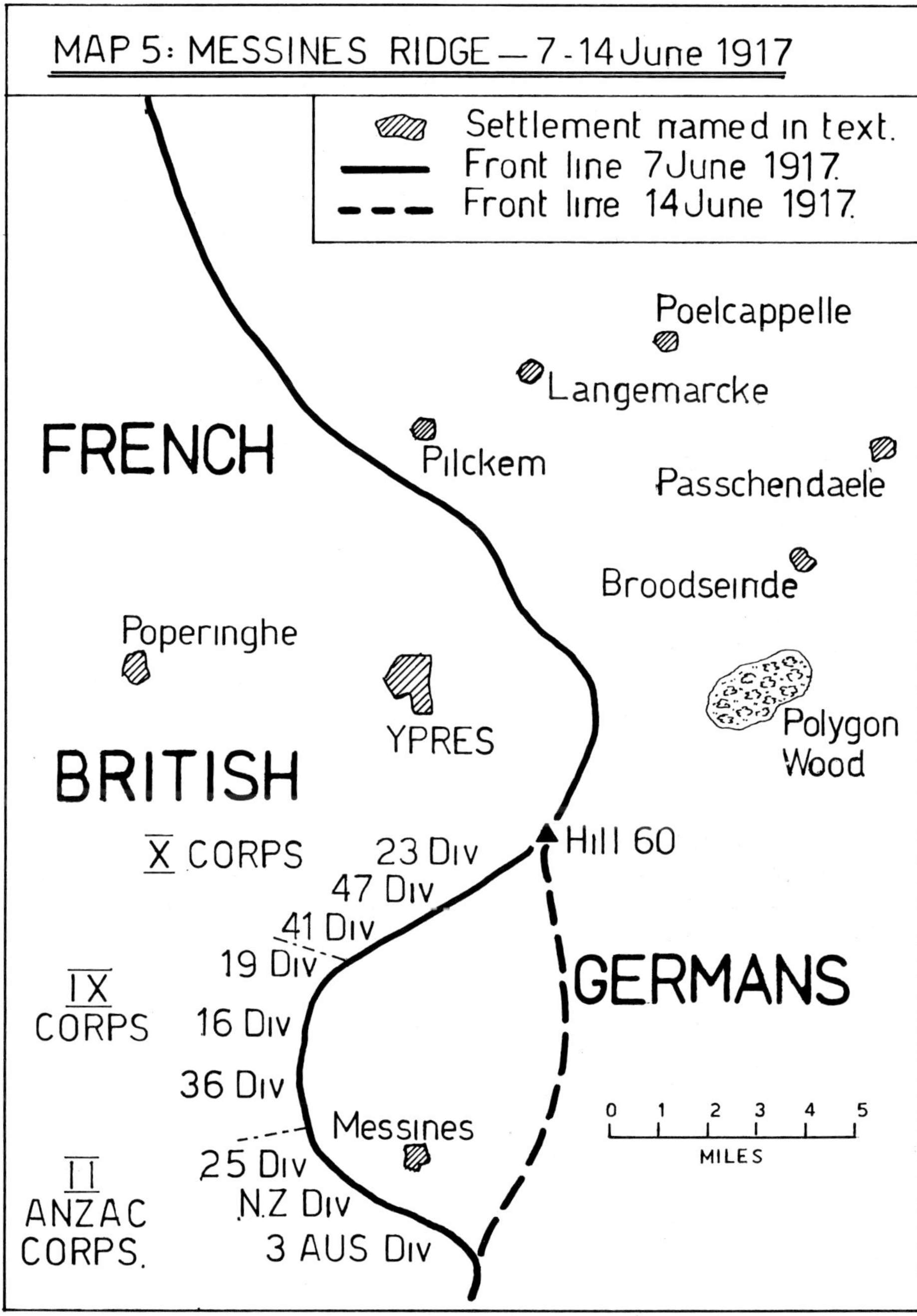
MAP 5: MESSINES RIDGE — 7-14 June 1917
Settlement named in text.
Front line 7 June 1917.
Front line 14 June 1917.
Poelcappelle
Langemarcke
FRENCH
Pilckem
Passchendaele
Broodseinde
Poperinghe
YPRES
Polygon Wood
BRITISH
X CORPS
23 Div
47 Div
41 Div
19 Div
Hill 60
IX CORPS
16 Div
GERMANS
36 Div
Messines
0 1 2 3 4 5
MILES
II ANZAC CORPS.
25 Div
N.Z Div
3 AUS Div

> even where I was three miles away. And immediately all our guns seemed to blaze forth destruction. I took my men down to a dump right among them and it was an experience."
> WE 23rd. June, 1917.

The British artillery fire had been kept normal during the night and had fallen silent just before the explosions (so much so that in the front line nightingales could be heard singing in the woods to the rear) but now the whole of its strength was let loose at its maximum rate of fire.

> "There seemed to be thousands of them (guns) of all kinds and I'm sure nothing could have lived under the bombardment."
> LJ 13th. July, 1917.

The terrific shock of the mine explosions had a demoralising effect beyond all expectations. Stunned and dazed Germans wandered about and were taken prisoner in their hundreds.

> "Early in the morning the prisoners started to come in and we asked them how they liked the explosion. They showed us how they fell on the floor and didn't know where they were for a while. They all looked shell-shocked and glad to be out of it."
> LJ 13th. July, 1917.

And:-

> "At about 4.30 a.m., prisoners began to come in and were they a happy lot! They are thankful to be caught, We have got a fine haul. Some of them speak good English. I went round to the dressing station later. It was pitiful. Friend and foe mixed up together, Germans carrying British and British carrying Germans. The Germans had begged to be allowed to help. All might have belonged to one army. One German officer was badly wounded and lay outside. On some German soldiers being asked to carry him, they refused saying let him die he turned the machine guns on us when we surrendered."
> WE 23rd. June, 1917.

Some indication of the manner in which the Germans had been caught by surprise by the explosions is given in a letter from a Leigh soldier, Private Ellison:-

> "I saw some dead Germans with their hands in their pockets, some sitting round a table (obviously killed by the shock waves) and some even without their boots on."
> LC 21st. December, 1917.

Constable Beattie took time off from directing traffic in the rear echelons and went forward to see for himself:-

> "I had a look at the place yesterday and it was the sight of a lifetime to see the way our artillery had shattered his trenches, you would think that a huge earthquake had taken place. There are some craters which would hold a large ship. (here he was looking at the mine craters) and all about are strewn rifles, bayonets, overcoats and some black bread. I saw a few dead lying about."

Behind a creeping artillery barrage which lifted 100 yards every two minutes over 80,000 men swamped the German defences. Gone were the endless lines of slowly advancing men which had been mown down at the Somme in 1916. Instead small assault groups using mortars, Lewis guns and grenades rushed forward to overrun or outflank the German machine gun nests. This new method which had proved so successful for the Canadians at Vimy Ridge in April, 1917, included 'mopping up' parties to the rear which cleared captured defences of enemy stragglers. The German trenches were swiftly overwhelmed before unshaken reserves could be brought forward. By nine o'clock, the attacking troops were established along the entire length of the crest of Messines Ridge. There had been a difficult moment when the advance was held up by a German strong point which had somehow survived the holocaust, Sergeant John O'Shea from Ashton-in-Makerfield, who although only 24 years old had seen service in India, Gallipoli, Egypt and the Somme, single handedly eliminated it earning himself the D.C.M.

Thousands of British and Anzacs crowded the ridge summit and began to dig in. Only a fraction of the expected fifty percent casualities had been incurred so that there was unforseen congestion. It was now that the heaviest casualties occurred among the troops packed on the ridge as under cover of an artillery barrage the German counter-attack began. The British artillery advanced to support the newly won positions and Driver R. Croft Williams from Downall Green, in civilian life a grocer's assistant in Naylor's shop, Wigan Road, Ashton-in-Makerfield, moved into a forward observation post from which to

report to his battery. The German artillery constantly cut the telephone wire and three times Driver Williams volunteered to go back into the former No-Man's-Land, risking his life amid the falling shells in order to repair the wire. Justifiably he was awarded the Military Medal for his courage.

Another artilleryman, Corporal Jack Heyes from Warrington Road, Ashton-in-Makerfield, only 21 years old and a miner at Boston Colliery, Haydock, was not so lucky. With an officer he went forward to choose a new site for his battery as it advanced to give supporting fire to the attacking infantry. They were caught by a shell burst and both were killed. Yet another local man in the artillery, Gunner Peter Yates, whose father, Thomas Yates, owned a draper's shop in Ormskirk Road, Newtown, Wigan, was hit in the leg by a small fragment and although it was amputated in an attempt to save his life, he died the next day.

The battlefield was not an orderly straight line, confusion reigned as the two sides intermingled and there were several unfortunate, even disastrous events. Great care had to be taken by the artillery in order to avoid hitting their own men but several unfortunate incidents still occurred, One was on the 18th. June, 1917 when a British shell fell short and exploded in a trench of the 16th.Manchesters, killing Private Herbert Parkes of Billinge Road, Highfield, Wigan, an incident which is nowadays euphemistically termed 'friendly fire'. Not so friendly.

Private James Gradwell of the Field Ambulance Corps had just returned to the front after spending nine days' furlough in his home town of Leigh, his first leave for over two years, just in time to take part in the offensive. He was detailed to go up to the front line on stretcher bearer duties.

> "It is no easy work to carry a man a mile and sometimes two and three miles. When we get more away from the shell-swept ground we put the wounded on to the wheeled stretchers. Before 7th. June, my mates and I were followed by shells along the road because Fritz had the position where he could see us but that is taken from him and how well we know it."
> LJ 13th. July, 1917.

It was dangerous work on the opening day of the offensive and Gradwell's unit had seven or eight men wounded and half a dozen killed including his captain. Indeed, the work of the medical services during the First World War has often been understated. Private John

Walsham, RAMC, also from Leigh wrote of his duties in a casualty clearing station close to the front line:-

> "We act as go-between for the field ambulances and the base hospitals. We receive the sick and wounded from the trenches and hold them until they are fit to travel down to the base or to be returned to their own units. We are four miles behind the firing line so we are well within shell range. A few have landed near us and Fritz has also been busy with his aircraft and a few bombs have been dropped between the tents but no damage done. Our station will hold abut 400 0r 500 patients at once and has a staff of nine officers, seven sisters and a hundred NCO's and men who have to do and attend to all the patients. We commence duties at seven a.m., have half an hour for dinner and tea, finish at eight with lights out at nine thirty, three hours off duty each alternate day so it is hard going."
> LJ 16th. September, 1917

Walsham went on to recall a poignant example of the hospital's conditions:-

> "It is very trying at times for the patients plead for things they should not have and it seems cruel to refuse them but it is for the best. I remember one case particularly well. It was an abdominal case and he pleaded with me so hard for a cigarette which would have caused him great pain, but eventually the sister gave him one but it was not to be lighted. Every time we passed his bed he asked for a match and it was so hard to refuse for he was in so much agony at the time and the poor fellow died before morning. Some people say your only RAMC but you would be surprised at the number of patients who tell me they wouldn't have our job at any price. But someone has to do it."

Although the battle stuttered on for another six days, by dusk on the 7th. June, a sweeping British victory was already apparent. All objectives had been gained and the Germans had suffered enormous losses of men and material, some 19,900 casualties including 7,354 prisoners with 48 guns, 218 machine guns, 60 trench mortars also captured.

BRITISH CASUALTIES

	IX	X	IIANZAC
Officers killed	24	67	7
wounded	166	228	293
missing	0	5	8
Other ranks killed	627	3972	1714
wounded	3349	4787	8904
missing	1097	538	1396
Total	5263	6597	12391

Despite the emphatic victory there were over 24,000 allied casualties, half of them in the II ANZAC Corps, almost all of them a result of the overcrowding in the captured positions. However the way had been prepared for a decisive advance. The Somme had been avenged.

CHAPTER FOUR - THE MAIN BATTLES BEGIN.

Pilckem Ridge, 31st. July - 2nd. August, 1917.

A month's pause between the capture of Messines Ridge and the next stage of the attack on Pilckem Ridge had little bearing on the battle. The Germans knew where the next blow would fall, but a six-day postponement from 25th. to the 31st July proved disastrous. Officially the reason given for the delay was the need to bring up all the artillery and the slowness of the French, but the result was a prolonged artillery barrage and a further churning up of the ground over which the attacking infantry had to advance.

This time the British artillery numbered 2,299 field guns and howitzers which fired 4,283,550 shells, surpassing the total at Messines almost two months earlier. This bombardment marked the zenith of British protracted set-piece artillery barrages. Never again was there massive saturation shelling of German defensive positions prior to an attack. Later battles of the Passchendaele campaign proved that short concentrated bombardments sufficient to stun the defenders while attackers moved swiftly at them were an equally effective method at a fraction of the expenditure in shells and without destroying the ground over which the attackers had to cross.

Once more the Germans were shaken by the ferocity of the artillery barrage:-

> "In the early morning of the 31st. July a storm of fire broke out the like of which had never been experienced before. The whole of Flanders seemed to be in flames."
> von Kuhl 'Die Weltkreig 1914-18.'

The bombardment was not all one-way. As British preparations grew in intensity the Germans retaliated, pouring shells into Ypres, as many as ten thousand in one night. Colonel Rettie, commanding a battery in the field artillery brigade attached to the 55th. (West Lancashire) Territorial Division wrote in his diary:-

> "One of the worst months the brigade ever had to deal with was June, 1917. For three weeks Ypres became a perfect hell for us and anyone who left the protection of gun-pit or dug-out did so at the peril of his life. As for the drivers, it is a wonder that any transport got through at all."

THE PASSCHENDAELE CAMPAIGN - 1917

BATTLE	June	July	August	Sept:	October	Nov:
Messines Ridge	7–14					
Pilckem Ridge		31–	2			
Langemarcke			16–18			
Menin Road				20–25		
Polygon Wood				26–	3	
Broodseinde					4	
Poelcappelle					9	
1st. Passchendaele					12	
2nd. Passchendaele					26–	11

Samuel Price of Holt Street, Westleigh was mentioned in despatches after a trench raid on the night of 29th/30th. July to discover the bombardment's effectiveness. Only a small man, five feet four inches, he had enlisted in the 'Bantam' Company of the 20/Lancashire Fusiliers early in 1916. Miraculously he went through the war in the trenches unscathed, only hospitalised once when he was hit in the leg by shrapnel when resting in the rear echelon!

On the eve of the offensive Colonel Rettie confided more thoughts to his diary:-

> "I put on my gas mask and went outside, It was weird beyond description, a bright moonlight but a haze of smoke, gas and brick dust hung above the town. Near us the gable end of a ruined church stood above the welter of rubble. Now and again the burst of a shell lit up the ruins with a lurid glare while the whine of the gas shell, the scream of the others, the crash of their burst and the sound of falling bricks were continuous."

As the time of the offensive approached Rettie continued:-

> "It is a weird sensation waiting for those last few moments before zero hour. There is a tense feeling in the air. It even seems to affect the telephone. But what of the infantry waiting to go over the top? Theirs is a very different sort of wait, lying in the mud thinking of what is in front of them."

At zero hour the infantry went over the top. Waves of attackers swamped the German defences with small groups of men behind them mopping up any enemy pockets left behind. Within a few hours the leading infantry reached the crest line of the Pilckem Ridge and captured the forward German observation points overlooking the Ypres Salient.

One Wigan man, before the war a cotton mill clerk, now serving in a Scottish Regiment, wrote home:-

> "Everyone went over the top as if they were rehearsing behind the lines instead of the real thing. Most of the lads (including myself) had never been over the top before which made it all the more creditable. But the chief factor was the magnificent artillery we had behind us. The Boche hadn't a ghost of a chance given the barrage of our artillery that day. It was marvellous."
> WO 21st. August, 1917.

MAP 6: PILCKEM RIDGE—31 July - 2 August 1917

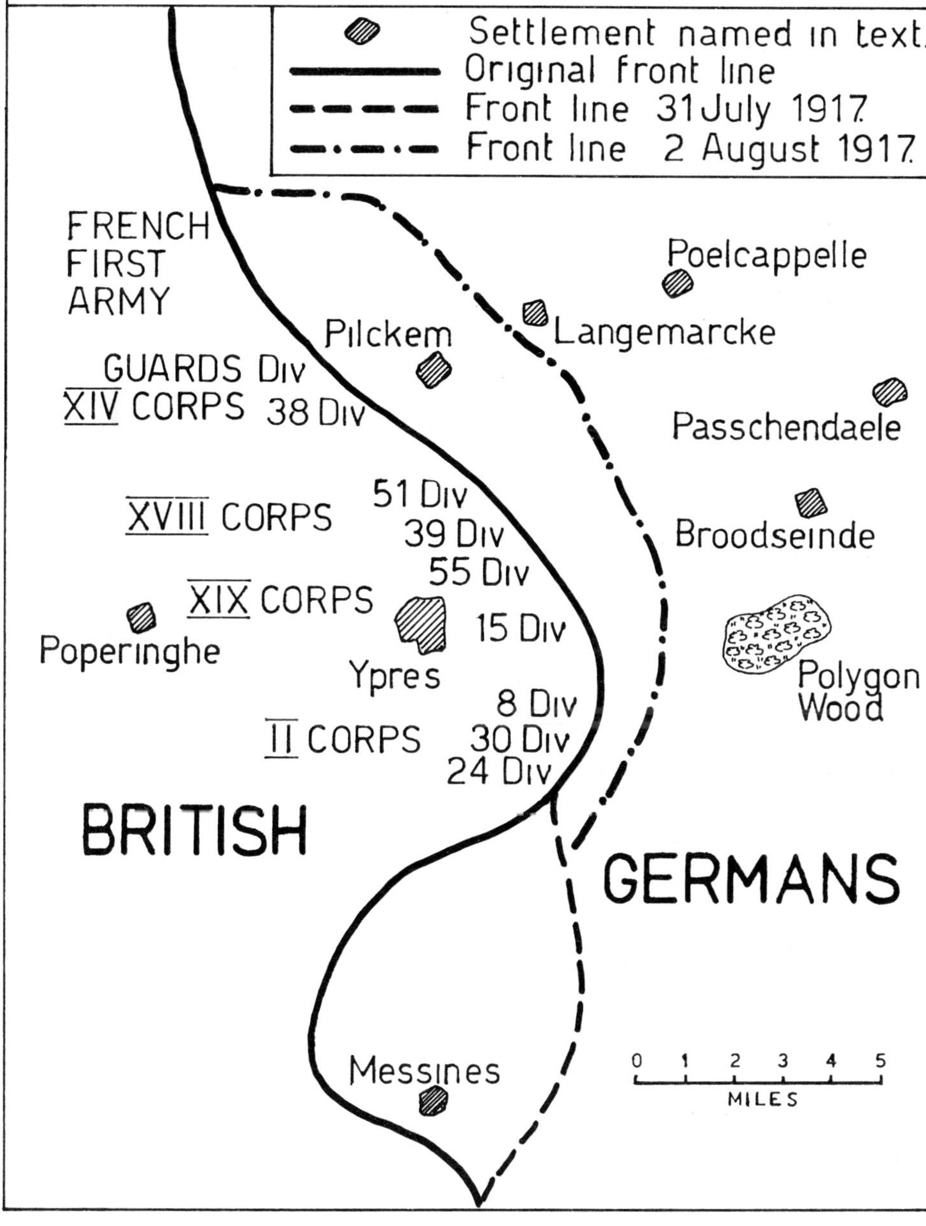

Another Wigan soldier, signing off as 'Alex', wrote home to his parents:-

> "This was the biggest battle since war broke out. It was awful and at the same time wonderful. We crept to within a few yards of the Germans and dug ourselves into a shell hole for protection while we waited for the signal to attack at dawn. At last the grey dawn appeared in the east and every minute seemed like an hour. All of a sudden thousands of our guns opened out and it was like being in Hell for the whole sky was a mass of flame and one could see to pick a match up after being in darkness a few minutes before. We then went though fire and water to get at the Hun as quickly as possible and in a few ticks we had them howling for mercy at the point of the bayonet. We captured and killed all of the first line and continued to advance through a Hell on earth and if I shouted an order a man could not hear me the noise was so great.
> We went another hundred yards or so and we were held up with some snipers and machine gun fire. We soon worked round and rushed the position killing all in it for they had caused us a lot of casualties. After that, we went forward and the first thing we dropped on were some live Huns in a dugout. God knows what damage they had been doing. They were that frightened when we rushed them and that cowardly that they could not move. I had to jab them with my bayonet to get them to move. They were young, seventeen or so and sent back as prisoners.
> We kept advancing on and on, rushing everything in front of us for four or five miles (sic). At night we were relieved and went out of the line for a rest. This morning I am in camp with twelve of my men and the rest are out of action. I am sick, sore, tired, weary and war-worn but I am all right now I have had a sleep and a feed. Thank God I have been lucky. Someone is watching over me."
> WE 8th. September, 1917.

Private Harold Wilkinson from Mosley Common also had a close shave. Between eight and nine hundred of his regiment, the King's Royal Rifles, found themselves surrounded. Wilkinson was in his company's sniping section and with a comrade he opened up a way through for his regiment by, as the citation states, 'effective sniping'. Shortly afterwards he was buried for three and a half hours by a shell burst which killed the three men next to him. When he was dug out he was informed that he had been recommended for the Military Medal.

The battle was a baptism of fire for more local men, territorial soldiers in the 55th (West Lancashire) Territorial Division. Their position was north east of Ypres with the village of Passchendaele, its church clearly visible, about 7,000 yards ahead.

55th Division

Brigade	**Battalion**	**Origin**
164th.	1/4 King's Own Loyal Lancaster Regiment	Ulverston
	1/8 King's Liverpool (Irish) Regiment	Liverpool
	2/5 Lancashire Fusiliers	Bury
	1/4 Loyal North Lancashire Regiment	Preston
165th	1/5 King's Liverpool Regiment	Liverpool
	1/6 King's Liverpool Regiment	Liverpool
	1/7 King's Liverpool Regiment	Liverpool
	1/9 King's Liverpool Regiment	Liverpool
166th.	1/5 King's Own Loyal Lancaster Regiment	Lancaster
	1/10 King's Liverpool (Scottish) Regiment	Liverpool
	1/5 South Lancashire Regiment	St. Helens
	1/5 Loyal North Lancashire Regiment	Bolton
Pioneers	1/4 South Lancashire Regiment	Warrington

An observer who watched the Lancashire territorials go forward, later wrote to his local paper:-

> "To these men it fell to advance over some of the most exposed and sodden ground on the whole of the battle area. There was often nothing whatever to guide them towards those spots on the shell-tossed wire-tangled monotony which formed their objectives according to the plan. The wind was blowing a gale and visibility was poor. The struggling khaki-clad figures so blended into the dreary hue of the landscape that it was frequently difficult to detect them."
> WO 13th. October, 1917.

He watched, mesmerised as they pressed forward:-

> "The advance would be made across an oozy wilderness with not a German in sight then suddenly our lads would stumble on a camouflaged trench covered with muddied brushwood from which a sharp salvo would rattle forth. Along the Passchendaele

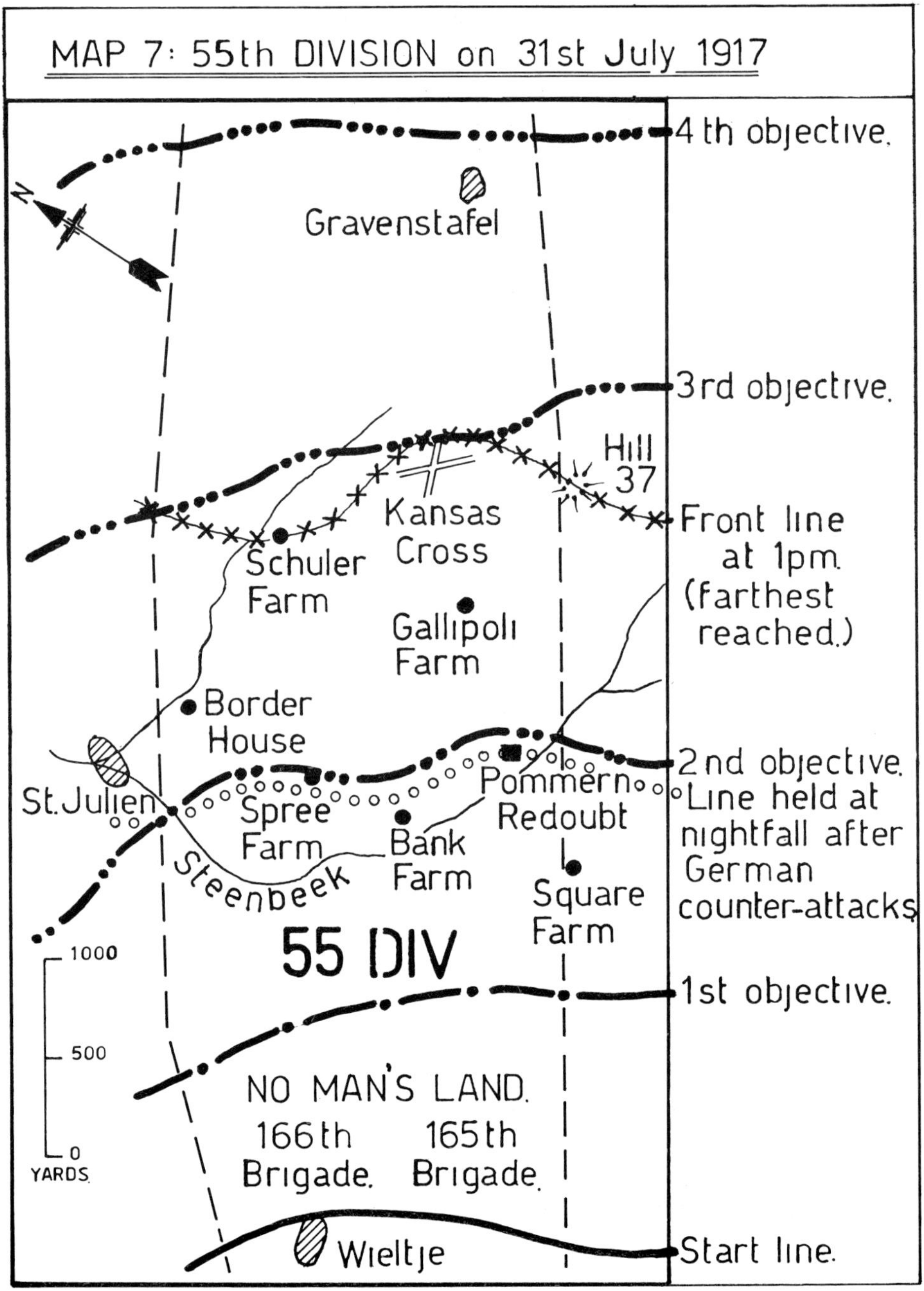
MAP 7: 55th DIVISION on 31st July 1917
4 th objective.
Gravenstafel
3rd objective.
Hill 37
Kansas Cross
Front line at 1pm. (farthest reached.)
Schuler Farm
Gallipoli Farm
Border House
2nd objective.
Line held at nightfall after German counter-attacks
St. Julien
Spree Farm
Pommern Redoubt
Bank Farm
Steenbeek
Square Farm
55 DIV
1000
500
0
YARDS.
1st objective.
NO MAN'S LAND.
166th Brigade.
165th Brigade.
Wieltje
Start line.

road the Germans would suddenly appear in numbers from behind concrete breastworks, dragging machine guns."
WO 13th. October, 1917.

In pouring rain, two brigades, 165th. and 166th., of the Lancashire territorials, crossed the Steenbeek stream but only after extremely stiff fighting. Several strongpoints stubbornly held out. Square Farm, a ruin with fortified cellars, Spree Farm, Bank Farm and Pommern Redoubt, resisted for up to three hours and were only captured when tanks arrived. A weak spot in the British artillery barrage had left these strongpoints intact. Taking over from their comrades, 164th Brigade continued up the slope towards the third and fourth objectives. Eventually the enemy third line was reached and a German battery which continued to fire at point-blank range (100 yards) was rushed and captured. Both leading battalions, (2/5 Lancashire Fusiliers and 1/5 Loyal North Lancashires) of the 164th., lost more than half of their strength and the two support battalions were merged with them.

Rain continued into the early afternoon as the expected German counterattack began, an intense artillery barrage, followed by six waves of infantry assisted by low flying planes, machine gunning and dropping bombs, one of the earliest examples in military history of such close ground-support by aircraft. The hastily formed British defensive line was over-run and 164th brigade reluctantly fell back through their hard-won gains eventually consolidating in the captured German second line with the men who had captured it. The Germans hurled themselves forward and were mown down in droves but the inexperienced 55th Division had lost heavily, 164th. Brigade losing seventy percent of its strength and having to be taken out of the line.

BRITISH CASUALTIES [1]

	Officers	Other ranks
55TH DIVISION	160	3,287
(164 Brigade)	(70)	(1,300)

For a week prior to the assault the weather had been fine but throughout the battle it rained non-stop, forcing the British to struggle through mounds of dirt pitted with shell craters, hampered all the time by clinging mud, depriving them of a decisive victory.

[1]killed, wounded and missing.

One Wigan combatant realised how close the British had come to a breakthrough and how much the weather had held them back:-

> "It was a darned pity the rains came. It has rained practically every day since, turning the ground into a morass and impeded operations. Given favourable weather I think we should have been nearer peace than all the peace cranks can ever attain."
> WO 1st. September, 1917.

A trifle optimistic!

The low lying clay soil torn by shells and sodden with rain turned into a lake of deep, muddy ponds. The hollows became swamps, impassable except by a few trackways of planks and duckboards which were soon targeted by the German artillery. To stay on them invited shelling, to leave them risked death by drowning and indeed several men and pack animals were lost in that way. It took ten horses to pull a single artillery piece and thirty six horses to move a battery just one mile.

A general advance of three thousand yards had been made and while 31,850 causalities were half those of the opening day of the Somme[1], to which all battles were now being compared, they were still severe. It was small consolation that German losses were probably in excess. The British were only halfway to their final objectives and had already lost half of their effective fighting strength. Once more the assaulting divisions remained in the captured trenches exposed to enemy counterattacks. As British artillery barrages prepared for the next phase of the attack a correspondent noted:-

> "With the return of perfect weather and beautiful visibility the struggle all along the front has assumed great intensity. As I write, aeroplanes pass and repass overhead. The guns are never silent and looking up from my paper I can see great clouds of smoke from shellbursts. At some point in the back German area between me and the belfry of Bruges which is clearly visible in the transparent air, a white column of smoke rises and spreads slowly where our aeroplanes have set fire to a dump or some similar object."
> WE 14th. August, 1917.

[1]See companion volume "The Finest of All. Local Men on the Somme".

The writer continued, describing how the German counterattacks along Pilckem Ridge had been thrown back:-

> "The brunt of the latest fighting has been borne by the Lancashire Fusiliers and the Loyal North Lancashires and they have inflicted enormous losses on the enemy. Airmen who are the best authorities report that they had never seen the ground so strewn and heaped with German dead."

Not all fighting was during the day. Very often both sides clashed during the hours of darkness. Private Walter Brown of the Manchester Regiment, from Local Board Street, Ince, and before the war an accountant for Wigan Coal and Iron Company, found himself isolated and pinned down in a shell crater in No-Man's-Land. Gathering up items of abandoned equipment, helmets, water bottles and the like, he devised a plan to get back to his own lines unscathed. Throwing a tin helmet to the right he waited until the hidden German machine gun fired at the clattering noise before darting into the blackness to his left. He repeated this procedure, scattering equipment left and right until he stumbled back to the safety of his own trenches once more.

Langemarcke 16th. - 18th. August, 1917.

The incessant rain, the reason for the premature conclusion of the Pilckem Ridge attack, caused several postponements for the follow-up assaults so it was not until 4.45 a.m. on the morning of the 16th. August that another major effort was launched.

The state of the ground was by now, quite awful. The effort required to bring up ammunition and supplies or to move artillery which had sunk up to the axles in mud was exhausting. For the infantry who had to attack across waterlogged shellholes, movement was painfully, often fatally slow. Mopping up was complicated by the shell-holed area which provided nooks and crannies in which the German survivors could hide.

For two days the battle raged. The Germans made no attempt to hold an unbroken line of trenches instead defence was organised in isolated strongpoints supported firstly by immediate counter attacks in regimental strength, then within twelve hours a counter attack by a reserve division.

An Orrell soldier, before the war employed at Sandbrook cotton mill, wrote home:-

"Me and the Lewis gun team were in the first line and were in the German positions first. It was four in the morning when we went over and immediately we showed our heads over the parapet there was a continual stream of machine gun bullets flying about. I saw scores of our fellows put out but what there was left of us went on and reached the German snipers and it helped that we got round the back of them that had been and were knocking our fellows out. As soon as they were cornered they cried in the usual way, "Mercy Kamerad". I can tell you we gave them mercy with the Lewis gun and the bayonet. We had a good rum issue before we went out and that made us a bit frisky."
WE 24th. November, 1917

Only hours latter, the same soldier was lying wounded in a casualty clearing station when it was bombed by a German aeroplane:-

"With two shots they (British anti-aircraft fire) fetched him down not far away but the pilot did not live long after he touched the ground because he was put to sleep by the Australians."

Private F.S. Lee from Upholland won the D.C.M. in charge of another Lewis gun team. He was buried by a shell, extricated himself then dug out his men. Leaving shelter to help a wounded comrade, he was knocked over by a shellburst, Shortly afterwards he extinguished a heap of burning ammunition, but he only got one medal!

The German counterattacks were beaten off but not before their shelling had inflicted heavy casualties. Among those killed was twenty one year old Private William Hollingsworth who, before the war, had been a collier at St., George Pit, Tyldesley. He had made seventeen attempts to enlist but had been turned down each time because of his eyesight.

On 12th. September, 1917, in another German counter attack, an advanced post of the Irish Guards found itself surrounded. It held out for ninety six hours before the defenders decided to retreat. Private Thomas Woodcock, from Teck Street off Darlington Street East, Wigan, covered the retirement with a Lewis gun, only falling back when the enemy were within a few yards. Crossing a stream to safety, he heard shouts for help behind him, retraced his steps and rescued a wounded guardsman amid a shower of hand grenades. In clear view of the enemy he carried the wounded man back to the British trenches heedless of machine gun fire sprayed at him. For this act of 'conspicuous bravery and determination' (official citation), he was

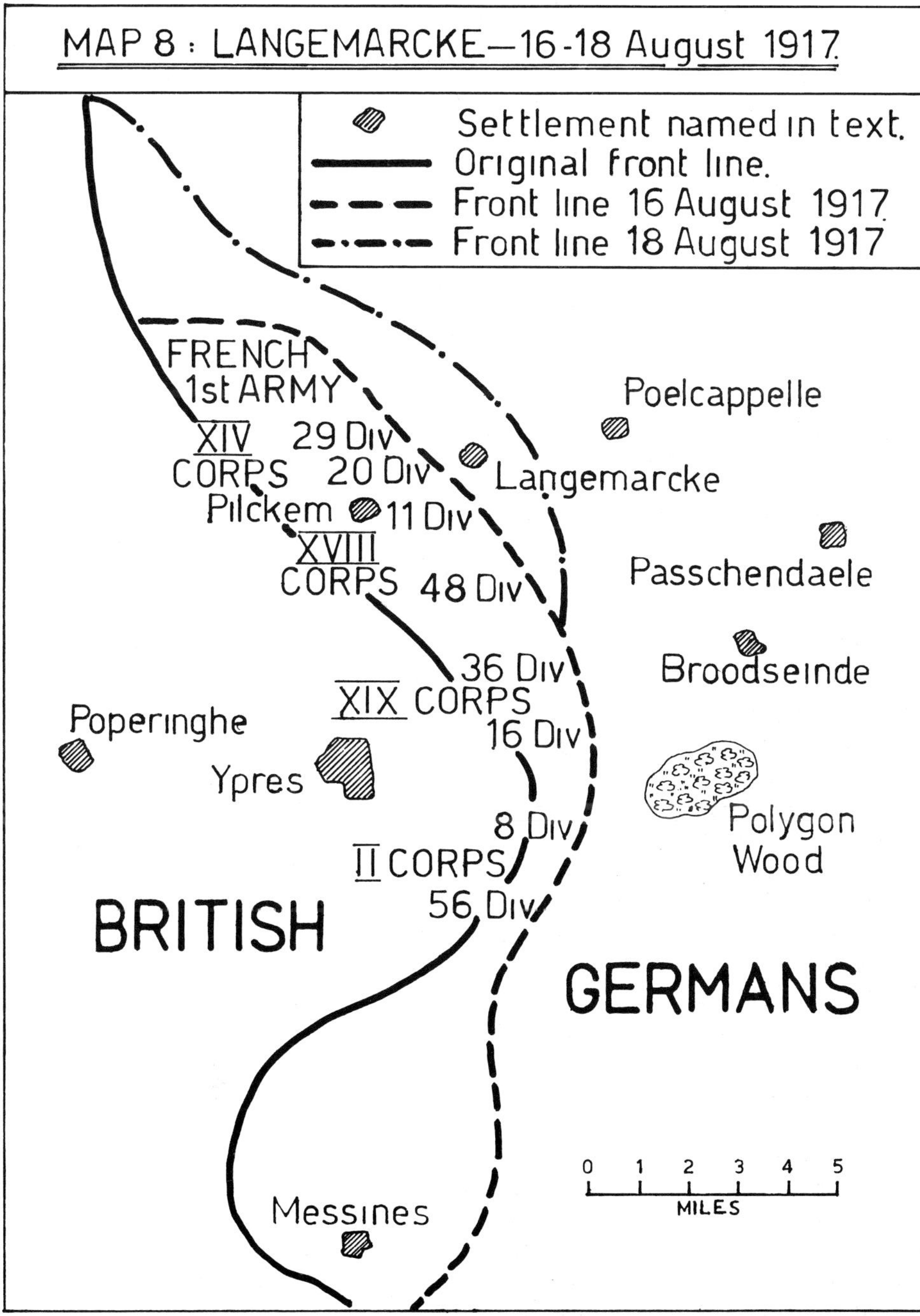
MAP 8 : LANGEMARCKE—16-18 August 1917
Settlement named in text.
Original front line.
Front line 16 August 1917
Front line 18 August 1917
FRENCH 1st ARMY
XIV CORPS
29 Div
20 Div
Pilckem
11 Div
XVIII CORPS
48 Div
Poelcappelle
Langemarcke
Passchendaele
Broodseinde
36 Div
XIX CORPS
16 Div
Poperinghe
Ypres
Polygon Wood
8 Div
II CORPS
56 Div
BRITISH
GERMANS
0 1 2 3 4 5
MILES
Messines

awarded the Victoria Cross, the highest honour for valour it is possible to win. Strictly speaking he was the Borough of Wigan's first Victoria Cross winner, two earlier recipients, Joseph Grimshaw and Joseph Kenealey came from Abram and Stubshaw Cross.[1]

Thomas Woodcock was typical of the soldiers produced by this district during the First World War. Born in Belvoir Street, Scholes, on leaving St. Patrick's R.C. Elementary School, he followed his father and two brothers into the mines. Although he was married with three children and his job gave exemption from military service he volunteered for the army in 1915 and by the year's end he was fighting in France. In February, 1918, he returned to Wigan on leave and next month was the guest of honour at a St. Patrick's Day dinner at his old school where in response to a speech in his praise he replied, *"I am going back to France tonight to do a bit more for the King."* Ten days later he was killed in action at Bullecourt in France.

At Langemarcke, the Germans fought stubbornly. It is still the site of their largest military cemetery in Belgium. German morale was holding and their army was nowhere near breaking point. The British high command was concerned that the lack of success so far was due to insufficient preparation, especially by artillery and for the next stage they drew up new plans.

[1]See companion volume 'Just Like Hell - Local men at Gallipoli'.

CHAPTER FIVE: STEP-BY-STEP ATTACKS.

As the situation in Russia rapidly worsened the transfer of German troops from the East to the Western Front seemed increasingly likely. French army discipline had not been fully restored and despite British Prime Minister Lloyd George's objections Haig was determined to continue the Flanders offensive. The new plan was a series of short, sharp assaults with strictly limited objectives. The intention was to take the rest of the plateau in four stages with an interval of six days between each one to give time to bring up artillery and more supplies. The length of each stage was restricted by the need to meet the strong German counterattacks using fresh attacking troops while still within effective range of supporting British artillery fire. Once more there was a delay following the previous offensive, this time one of over three weeks, the official reason being given as the need to construct roadways, establish telegraphic communications and bring up immense quantities of ammunition.

Building roads in the rear of the front line was vital yet unsung work requiring specialists, and much of it was done by companies of municipal workers brought out to France specially for that purpose. Corporal William Melling, formerly a road worker for Wigan Council wrote home:-

> "I find it far different from the home style. Our work consists chiefly of repairing roads that are not fit to carry traffic of a heavy character and make them fit to bear the enormous traffic necessary to maintain our army in the field. We have to make use of whatever material we can get, even using the rubble from the ruins left by the gentle Hun. We start at seven thirty in the morning and finish at half past four with a half hour break for dinner at noon. There are eight corporals in the company and we each have a working party of thirty, forty or sixty according to the nature of the work."
> WO 19th. August, 1817.

The Germans had been shelling the Menin Road for two years. Their gunners knew every yard, pinpointing every crossroad and junction. At night they searched the road for supply columns, pounding the surface into a mass of shellholes which miraculously the British roadworkers faithfully and patiently mended.

Constable Beattie gave an insight into his activities:-

> "I am on traffic duty in France. It is not a pleasant duty to perform when Fritz takes it into his head to put a few shells over. It is hard work, rough, bad, heavy roads and a few falls into the bargain."
> WO 4th. July, 1917.

Corporal Thomas Platt from Tyldesley, travelled through the rear areas up to the front when his unit was posted to France and was amazed at what he saw:-

> "Full gauge railways with big locomotives are within a few miles of the front line. Numberless motor vehicles of every type on roads, wide, splendid macadam roads, built for this traffic. We have an overwhelming number of guns and a greatly superior airforce. Everything here convinces me that we shall win."
> LJ 16th. March, 1917.

If the ordinary infantryman was so confident, is it any wonder that the high command, in possession of the total overall picture, was supremely confident too? Yet Platt adds an apprehensive note to his letter:-

> "We know the spring will bring victory, but at what cost! But we all agree the achievement will be worth it."

The superiority of the British war machine was now evident. British artillery dominated the battlefield as never before as the factories delivered guns and ammunition at a unprecedented rate. Although the numbers used, 1,295 field guns of all types, was less than at Pilckem Ridge, the narrow frontage made it the greatest artillery concentration seen so far in the war. Corporal Platt acknowledged the contribution of the munition workers:-

> "We appreciate the efforts at home. They keep down our casualties and it gives us confidence to hear our artillery put over ten to the Boche one."
> LJ 16th. March, 1917.

In addition the Royal Flying Corps had won superiority in the air and were helping their infantry on the ground. Private Frank Hayes from Wigan was able to show his appreciation when a British plane came down in No-Man's-Land and with a comrade from Haydock he braved the enemy's fire to bring in the wounded pilot. Hayes was awarded the D.C.M. but his pal, killed by a sniper, left a widow and three children.

Still the district's best known regiment, the 1/5 Manchesters, spent a fortnight in the trenches in front of Ypres during September, 1917. Following their evacuation from Gallipoli[1], they had served a spell in Egypt defending the Suez Canal then recruited, refitted and reorganised back in England, where, in June, 1916, a new officer arrived, Second Lieutenant Wilfred Owen, destined to be the finest poet of the First World War. Although from a middle class background, he had mixed extensively with the working classes but he seems to have received a severe culture shock on meeting the men in his new command and he didn't hide his feelings in a letter to his mother:-

> "The generality of the men are hard-handed, hard-headed miners, dogged, loutish, ugly, but I would trust them to advance under fire and to hold their trench. Coarse, ungainly, strong, indefatigable, unlovely Lancashire soldiers, Saxons to the bone."

In another letter to his brother he wrote:-

> "These rough, Lancashire lads are extraordinarily open, honest and incapable of deviousness."

All the time he spent with the 1/5 Manchesters, Owen was aware of his youth and military inexperience, and clearly embarrassed to be put in command of older men, most of them veterans, some recovering from wounds and to have to give them orders or to supervise them trench-digging. On one occasion he reprimanded a soldier for not having a toothbrush only to discover later that it had been lost on active service. A sensitive man, his diary recorded his acute discomfort. In December, 1916, the 1/5Manchesters moved to France but Owen was not destined to fight alongside men from this district. Heavy losses in the 2/Manchesters, especially among the officers caused his transfer to them.

The rush of volunteers to the ranks produced several more examples of culture shock as the local recruits, many of whom had never before in their lives travelled further than Blackpool, met men from all over the country and when in addition, the educated public school officers

[1]See companion volume 'Just Like Hell - Local men at Gallipoli'.

encountered working class Wiganers and Leighites for the first time! Old loyalties died hard. A smart sentry from Wigan was commended by an officer who enquired, *'What company are you my man?'* The reply came promptly, *'Wigan Coal and Iron Company, Sir!'*

A musketry instructor was pleased with the accuracy of one Leigh recruit but puzzled by the rifleman's remark that his shooting was *'awl reet'*.A comrade translated for the officer who wondered what the man would say if he was not pleased? *'It's awl rung, Sir.'*

Another Wigan recruit paraded without his regulation bayonet. On being asked by the inspecting officer where it was, he replied, *'Ah've getten noan.'* Perplexed by this the officer looked at the next man, also from Wigan for an explanation. The recruit leaned across and whispered conspiratorially, *'Ee means ees baht.'*

The enlisted men often had difficulty comprehending each other. One local recruit complained to his sergeant that he couldn't understand most of the others in his billet. 'They're speaking Welsh,' he was told *'Thi mitt as weel bi spekin Klondike,'* came back the reply.

In the difficult conditions underground it was not easy for the miners to keep a sense of humour but the chance came when 253rd. Tunnelling Company heard a German working a few yards ahead of their tunnel. Laying an explosive charge they blew him up. *'Yon mon's workin' wi an 'harp nah, captain norr a spade,'* confided the Wiganer sapper.

It was when the Wiganers met the Germans that there was a real clash of attitudes. Over three hundred local men were taken prisoner during the war and many had harrowing experiences to tell on their return. Two men gave extensive interviews to the local press. John Woodhall from Gidlow Lane had been a regular soldier 1901-7 followed by seven years as a reservist and on the outbreak of war he was called up from his job as a driver with Wigan Corporation. He was in the early fighting and was taken prisoner on 31st. October, 1914 at Zillebeke, just east of Ypres.

> 'They marched us off beating us with the butt end of their rifles. The first day they gave us three little biscuits and a cup of water. We were packed into cattle trucks, sixty to a truck and we were on the train wounded and everybody together for three days. The train stopped at every station so the German civilians could have a good look at us. Ask them for a drink of water and they spat at you. Even their Red Cross nurses did that. At the lager (camp) they gave us black bread, soup that tasted worse than cabbage water and burnt barley coffee.
> WO 14th. January, 1919.

Woodhall gave a graphic description of the brutal treatment meted out to the Russian prisoners who were *'beaten and murdered every day'* and were shot when they tried to escape. He was forced to work in all kinds of weather and ended up in a coal mine in southern Poland for half a mark (sixpence), two and half pence in todays money, a day.

Corporal James Fleming from Chapel Street, Wigan was one of six brothers to fight in the war. Another reservist, he too was called up immediately hostilities commenced and was wounded and captured on 8th. November, 1914. He too was beaten and fed scraps of food and forced to drink water out of buckets. Almost immediately on arrival at the camp, typhus broke out and their German guards abandoned them and set up a new perimeter two hundred yards away. For a year they existed on their own with no German doctors and if there had not been British doctors with them, Fleming believed they would have died. When he refused to work the Germans, *'kicked me like a football.'*

The locals in captivity never lost their sense of humour, an attribute which the Germans completely failed to appreciate:-

> "We would cheer loudly at any announcement by the camp authorities no matter what it was. A German who announced a reprisal for some misdemeanour was cheered by all present. Annoyance and doubling the punishment only led to increased cheering. We treated their notices of spurious victories in the same way. On every troop train that passed our camp they sang their national anthem. They couldn't understand why we sang 'Tipperary' back at them."
> WO 8th. March, 1919.

German exasperation at the British sense of humour was quite justified in an incident described by Lance Corporal J. Mallin of 3, James Street, Wigan, writing from his hospital bed in Ashton-under-Lyne where he was recovering from speech loss through shell-shock:-

> "I and four others were holding this sap which was only seventeen yards from the enemy sap and we had it pretty hot for a few hours when Fritz shouted across in broken English, *'You throw no bombs. We throw no bombs'*. So they threw us a tin of pork over and we threw them a tin of bully beef. Then they threw some cigars and we threw them some tins of jam and we kept doing this for about twenty minutes when our officer, noticing we were quiet, came to see what was wrong. When we saw him coming up the sap one of our lads picked up an empty jam tin, put

a bomb in it and lit it. Then he shouted across, *'Catch this Fritz'*, and threw it. Four of them put their hands up over the parapet to catch what they thought was a tin of jam. When the bomb exploded we could see arms and legs flying in the air and they shouted across to us, *'You bastard English swine,'* and it got hot again for a bit. The officer wanted to know why they had started bombing again so suddenly and we told him that they must have seen him coming up the sap but I don't think he believed us though he said nothing."
WE 3rd. October, 1916.

From March to August, 1917, the 1/5Manchesters refortified the British positions opposite the new German trenches on the Somme. Brigade headquarters was established in a ruined farmhouse near Havrincourt Wood and despite warnings that the building might be boobytrapped, the troops stripped the cellar of bricks and planks to make their dugouts. A few days later they were surprised when the farmer suddenly appeared, accompanied by two local gendarmes, two British Military policemen and carrying documents proving his ownership. Their amazement turned to despair when he dug up the cellar and unearthed several glass jars containing banknotes, coins and jewellery. Adding insult to injury, he cheerfully tipped a few francs to the British tommy who held the flickering candle which had provided the only light for the digger! For the rest of the war, whenever they captured or occupied a farmhouse, the Wiganers frantically dug up the cellar floor but without ever finding anything, at least to the knowledge of the regimental historian.

In September, 1917. the 42nd. Division was transferred to the Ypres Salient and on the first of that month, the entire unit, including the 127th. Brigade, which contained the 1/5 Manchesters, trudged through the ruined Menin Gate towards the front line, four miles away. Once the 'mud belt' was reached, the men had to follow their assigned duckboard track, 'F' painted in luminous letters so as to be legible at night, one of several radiating from Ypres. These signposted tracks were the only guides in the vast wilderness of mud where no trees, hedges, roads, or buildings remained and where there were no landmarks, no scraps of natural cover other than the mud-filled shell holes.

On 8th. September, the 1/5 Manchesters took over their allotted section of trenches where two days previously 126th. Brigade had attacked three German strongpoints and had been repulsed with the loss of 188 officers and men. This time there were to be no massed charges

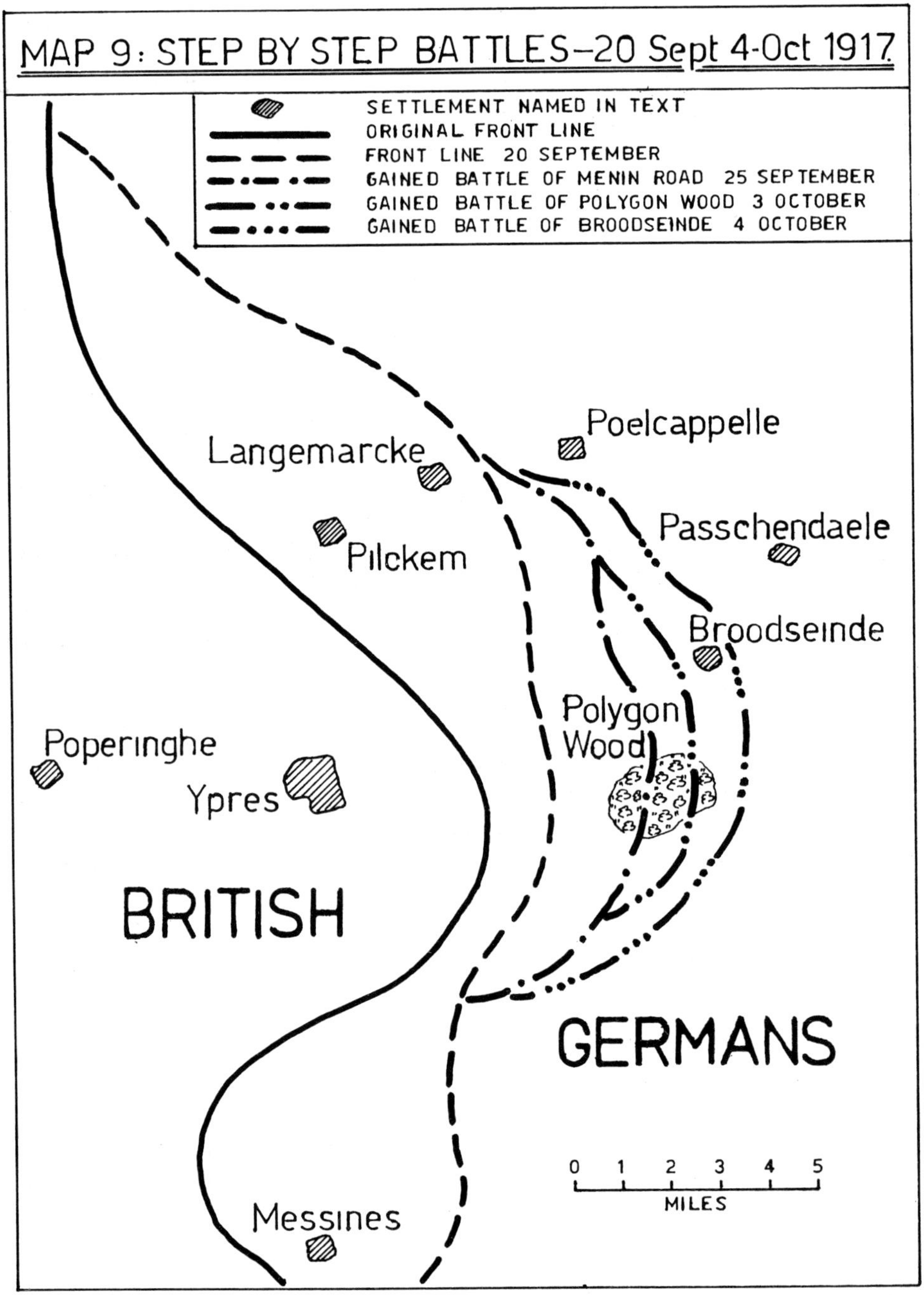
MAP 9: STEP BY STEP BATTLES–20 Sept 4-Oct 1917
SETTLEMENT NAMED IN TEXT
ORIGINAL FRONT LINE
FRONT LINE 20 SEPTEMBER
GAINED BATTLE OF MENIN ROAD 25 SEPTEMBER
GAINED BATTLE OF POLYGON WOOD 3 OCTOBER
GAINED BATTLE OF BROODSEINDE 4 OCTOBER
Poelcappelle
Langemarcke
Passchendaele
Pilckem
Broodseinde
Polygon Wood
Poperinghe
Ypres
BRITISH
GERMANS
0 1 2 3 4 5
MILES
Messines

for the 1/5 Manchesters similar to the those they had made against the Turks. Instead, they constantly patrolled No-Man's-Land to keep the Germans on the defensive. On the night of the 11th. September, 1917, a patrol found a wounded private of the Inniskilling Fusiliers who had been lying out in the open since 11th. August. Weak, he had survived by eating the rations scavenged from the dead bodies around him, and after being carried in by the Wigan soldiers, he subsequently recovered. On 15th, September, the 1/5Manchesters were relieved and went to a rear area for a rest.

The new British attacking methods were now expanded and perfected. As at Messines, lines of skirmishers led the attack, while behind them small groups took on enemy stongpoints and fortified shell holes. Following behind were more groups of mopping up parties. Each advance involved three components. The first objective was to be the longest, usually 800 yards and made by a weak force normally a battalion, just enough to overrun the thinly held German outposts. After a halt of forty five minutes for mopping up operations, a shorter advance of 500 yards was made by a fresh battalion. A longer halt of two hours at the second objective gave time to consolidate against German counter-attacks. The advance to the final objective was to be even shorter, 300 yards, and made by the two remaining battalions of each brigade which had been kept back for the purpose.

Pill-boxes were still the main German defence:-

> "He has got concrete dugouts where the nature of the land allowed him to make them and on lowlying ground he has reinforced concrete blockhouses or what they term them out here, 'pill-boxes'. That is the place where he has his machine guns and if our artillery misses any of them, they are the places that hold up our advance, Whenever we set out for an objective we usually get it but in some cases the casualties are somewhat heavy."
> WO 10th. November, 1917.

Menin Road 20th. to 25th., September, 1917.

The three-week delay had seen dry, sunny weather but overnight rain on the eve of the attack made the ground slippery yet four divisions advanced confidently as well they might. In front, they were screened to a depth of 1,000 yards by an unprecendented bombardment by the field artillery, together with a machine gun barrage and beyond all of this fell counter-battery fire, neutralizng the German batteries with gas and shell. The men had no difficulty in keeping up with the screen, indeed the main problem for the Australian officers was to stop their men from running through their own artillery barrage in their eagerness to get at the enemy! Just after ten o'clock, all three objectives had been taken. A letter home to Wigan had predicted why:-

> "The superiority of the artillery and I might add, the complete mastery we have in the war in the air, have enormously facilitated the attack."
> WO 1st. September, 1917.

The 55th (West Lancashire) Territorial Division was, in the words of the Official History to have:-

> "The most costly struggle of the day."

The division had lost 135 officers and 3,720 other ranks at Pilckem Ridge on the 31st. July and these casualties had not been properly replaced in fact about a thousand men arrived too late for the attack and had to be left behind. Early casualties resulted when an intense German artillery barrage crashed down as the division assembled in the jumping-off trenches. As they rose 'over the top' to follow their own barrage, they were swept by a hail of bullets from German machine guns and rifles at close range. Worse was to follow. The leading lines, moving through the early morning mist, failed to notice several dugouts and concrete strongpoints whose occupants emerged and blasted the supporting waves. Hearing the firing behind them the advance waves turned back and lost the cover of their creeping barrage. German artillery had cut the field telegraph wires, visual communication was impossible because of the mist and smoke, casualties among the runners were heavy. The division struggled forward and by noon had captured their first objective, a strong line of dugouts protected by barbed wire, but became hopelessly disorganised. By mid-afternoon when the German counterattack came the division had sorted itself out and re-established communications with their batteries. The attack was made by the German 459th Reserve Regiment. The regimental history describes its treatment by the Lancashire men:-

> "Every effort made to press the attack failed owing to the terrible artillery barrage and machine gun fire which tore great gaps in the advancing companies and caused complete disorganisation."

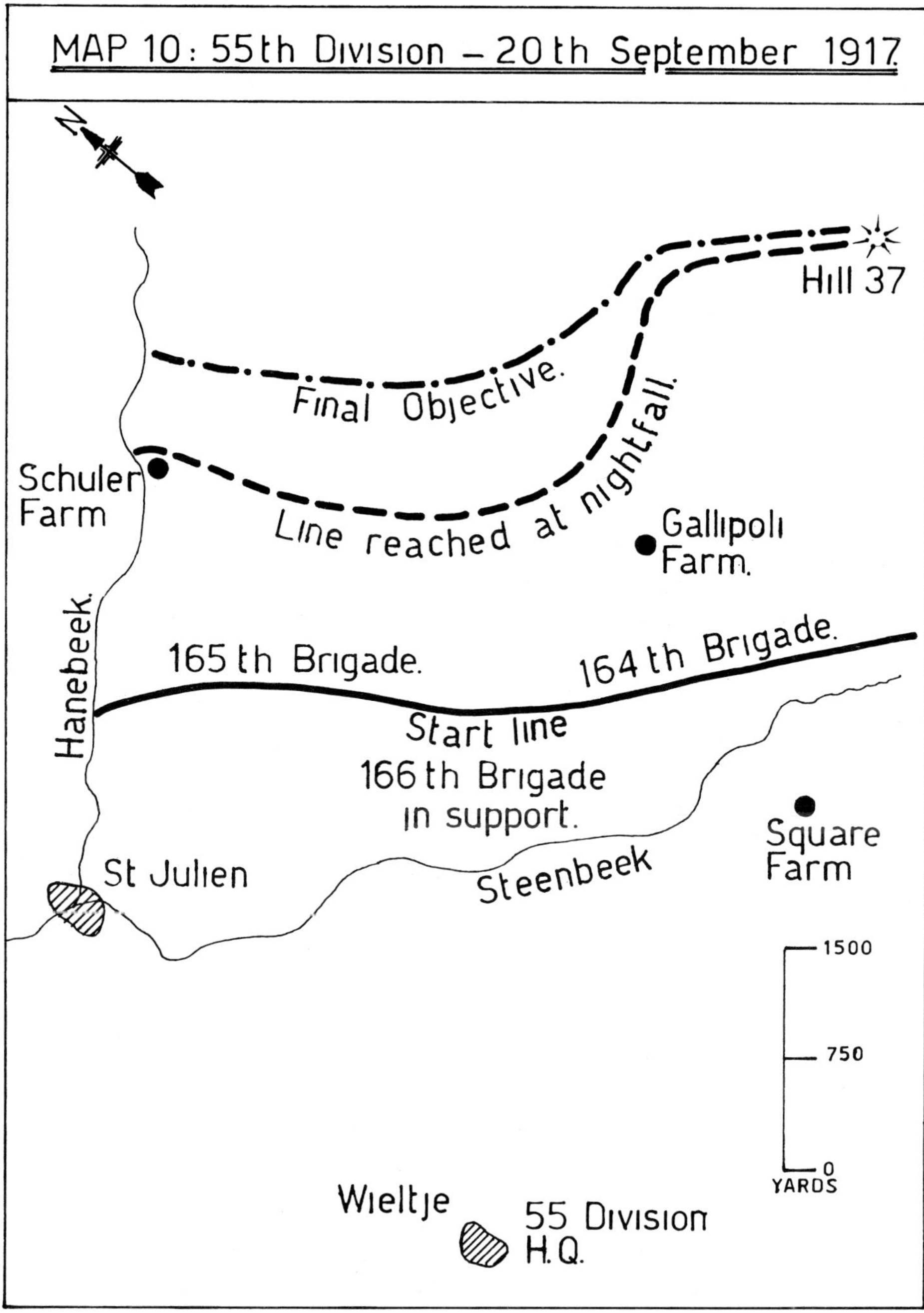
MAP 10: 55th Division – 20th September 1917
Hill 37
Final Objective.
Line reached at nightfall.
Schuler Farm
Gallipoli Farm.
Hanebeek.
165th Brigade.
164th Brigade.
Start line
166th Brigade in support.
Square Farm
St Julien
Steenbeek
1500
750
0
YARDS
Wieltje
55 Division H.Q.

Further German counter attacks were ripped to pieces. The new British methods had totally defeated the Germans' new defensive tactics. Once more, the casualties were high, over 20,000 men including 3,000 killed, especially in the 55th. Division:-

	killed	wounded	missing	total
Officers	27	78	7	112
Other ranks	143	1,507	182	1,832

As usual the casualties among the officers were higher proportionally (17%) than among the other ranks (13%). Nor were casualties confined to the infantry. The field artillery lost 51 officers (30%) and 690 other ranks (14%), while the heavy artillery lost 29 officers (20%) and 55 other ranks (15%). The machine gun sections did not escape unscathed with 58 officers (7%) and 537 other ranks (4%) casualties in which one in four were killed.

Polygon Wood 26th. September to 3rd. October, 1917.

Less than a week following this first stage success, seven divisions carried the line forward a further 1200 yards. Conditions underfoot were helped by another six days of dry weather, but the dust raised by the high explosive shells added to the smoke and early morning mist forced the attackers to keep direction by compass! Once more the price of victory was high, 15,000 causalities including 1,500 killed but German losses were higher at 19,000, a faster rate of losses than could be replaced, forcing the German High Command to revise their defensive tactics. Immediate counter attacks were abandoned and reserved for the next day.

Fighting had become a race against the weather. As autumn approached, the drying out strength of the sun lessened on the rain soddened landscape. Not only British headquarters were worried. A Wigan soldier wrote home anxiously:-

> "If we could only get fine weather we would show them the way!"
> WO 1st. September, 1917.

Broodseinde 4th. October, 1917.

After a week of fine weather, overnight rain reduced visibility to 30 yards, just as the third stage attack opened. As the infantry, mainly Australians, charged, they found Germans in every shell hole waiting to advance. The enemy had planned an attack for the very same time! Bitter hand-to-hand fighting took place in No-Man's-Land as the Australians chased the German survivors back to their own lines and beyond. With few exceptions, the main objectives were again taken. Once more the Germans suffered immense losses including another 4,000 prisoners. Three successful offensives within fifteen days! Everyone was elated. Preparations were made for the fourth and final hammer blow. Unfortunately disaster was about to strike.

Poelcapelle 9th. October, 1917.

After an interval of five days the offensive continued with the next blow planned for three days later. It rained steadily for all that time and his senior officers told Haig that, although willing to continue, they would prefer the campaign to end. Haig now had the bit between his teeth and ordered a continuance of the attacks, no doubt encouraged by the Australians, who begged that there should be no postponement. It was decided to attempt both steps in one day, a morning assault to reach half way, then bringing up replacements to reach the final objective 1,200 yards distant. It had rained all the fourth day, drizzle on the fifth had turned to showers on the sixth, with squalls on the seventh. Although it stopped on the eighth and there was a strong drying wind, by that evening it started again so that the assaulting brigades marched to their jumping-off positions through pouring torrents. Weather reports showed more storms approaching and no improvement in sight.

The assault troops had to march two and a half miles in darkness and in rain, struggling up to their knees in mud, constantly shelled by German artillery before they reached their jumping-off positions. Many units were late and there were huge gaps in the line. Worse still, the British barrage was, for once, ineffective. A large number of the guns failed to participate, others fired inaccurately from their unstable platforms, and many of the high explosive shells buried themselves harmlessly in the soft ground.

An onlooker recalled the scene:-

"Yesterday, during the battle, it was almost impossible to fly because of the gale and impossible to see. Even from points behind the front line, it was impossible to see anything of the men in the attack and difficult to get any exact knowledge of them for many hours."
WO 10th. November, 1917.

Behind the morass, machine guns in pill-boxes protected by barbed wire opened up on the men struggling towards them through the mud. Equally deadly were the snipers and machine gunners hidden in anonymous shell holes, the 'lonely man in the shell hole' of later German legend.

Yet more local territorials, this time the 66th. (East Lancashire) Territorial Division, received their baptism of fire. Their position was barely two thousand yards short of Passchendaele village, now a smouldering ruin its church spire long since gone.

66th DIVISION

Brigade	**Battalion**	**Origin**
197th.	2/6Lancashire Fusiliers	St. Helens
	2/7Lancashire Fusiliers	Salford
	2/8Lancashire Fusiliers	St. Helens
	3/5Lancashire Fusiliers	Bury
198th	2/4 East Lancashire Regiment	Blackburn
	2/5 East Lancashire Regiment	Burnley
	2/9Manchester Regiment	Ashton-under-Lyme
	2/10Manchester Regiment	Oldham
199th	2/5Manchester Regiment	Wigan
	2/6Manchester Regiment	Hulme
	2/7Manchester Regiment	Ardwick
	2/8Manchester Regiment	Ardwick
Pioneers	1/5Border Regiment	Cumberland

The 2/5Manchesters, Wigan's second territorial unit had been in France since February, 1917. On 3rd. November, they had filed through Ypres and the ruined Menin Gate, 34 officers and 835 men strong. rain falling in a steady drizzle and by nightfall had moved into their assigned positions[1] directly in front of Passchendaele, about 2,200 yards away.

[1]On roughly what is now Tyne Cot Commonwealth War Graves Commission cemetery.

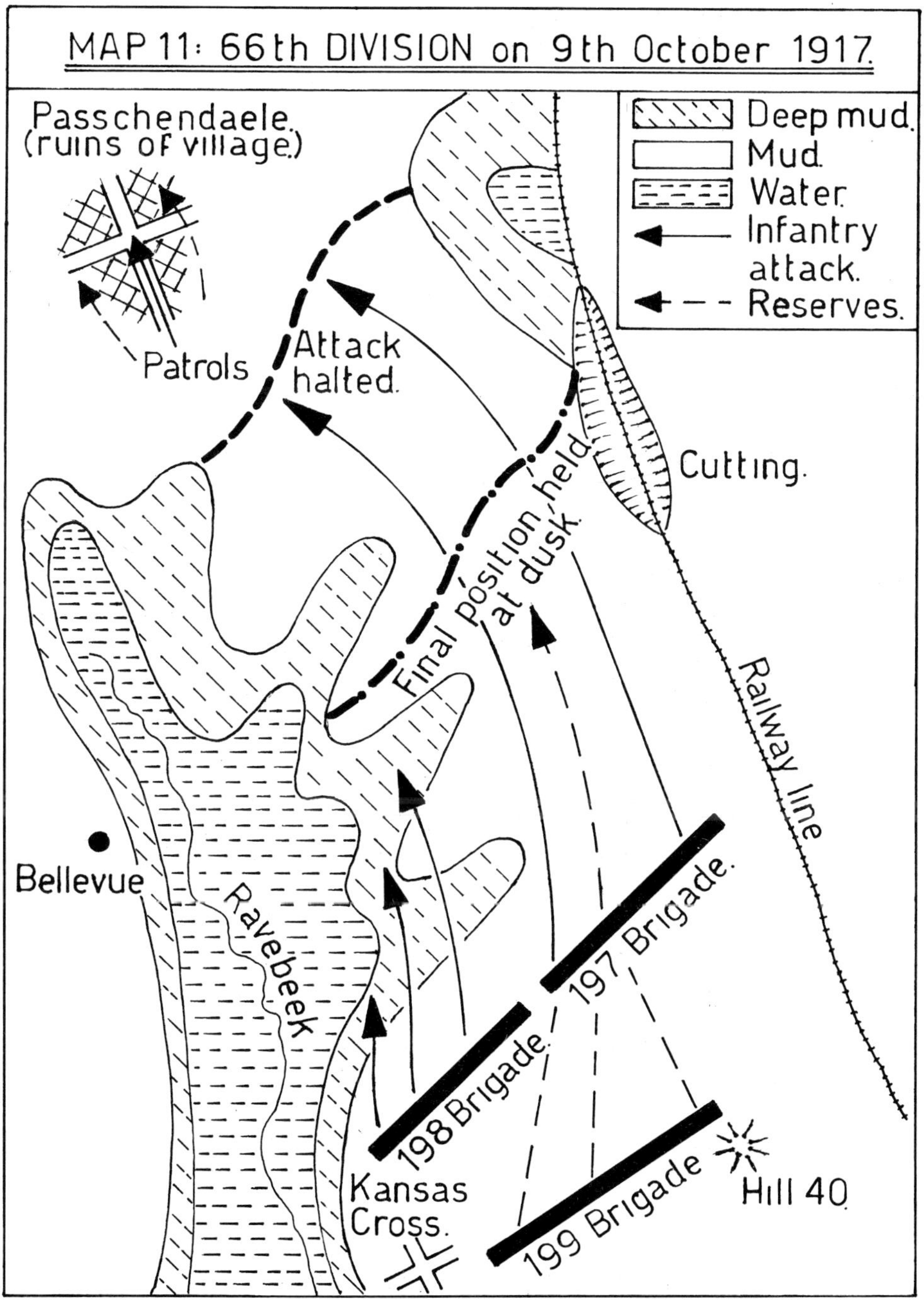
MAP 11: 66th DIVISION on 9th October 1917.
Passchendaele (ruins of village)
Patrols
Attack halted.
Deep mud.
Mud.
Water.
Infantry attack.
Reserves.
Cutting.
Final position held at dusk.
Railway line
Bellevue
Ravebeek
197 Brigade.
198 Brigade.
199 Brigade
Kansas Cross.
Hill 40.

Six days later they attacked. From 5.20 a.m. until 10.27 a.m., the artillery laid on its barrage. For four minutes it plunged down 150 yards ahead of the waiting infantry then for 200 yards it advanced at the rate of 100 yards in 4 minutes, with the next 100 yards in 6 minutes and the final 100 yards to the first objective in 8 minutes. Unfortunately there were huge gaps in the artillery screen.

The 330th. Brigade Royal Field Artillery managed to get 25 guns into action but about a mile to the rear of their intended position. Its companion battery, the 331st., did not get into position until the attack had moved forward. At their extreme elevation, 6,000 yards, the British guns found the German batteries behind Passchendaele to be well out of range and undisturbed, the German artillery hammered mercilessly at the advancing infantry.

About midnight, sleet began to fall as the troops were being pushed forward to the start lines, irrespective of their units. The 197th. Brigade attacked on the right with the 198th on the left with the 199th. in reserve.

Rain fell relentlessly as the Lancashire soldiers advanced bravely forward. On the left, 198th brigade's progress was held up by thick mud, derelict waterlogged trenches and the swollen Ravebeek stream. As the brigade struggled along, enfilade fire from three uncaptured pill-boxes on their left pulled them up still 300 yards short of their objective. On the higher, drier ground to the right, 197th. Brigade made better progress and reached the day's final objective, 300 yards short of Passchendaele village. A patrol of the 2/8 and 3/5 Lancashire Fusiliers even entered the ruined village where scattered groups of Germans sheltering in shell holes, quickly surrendered. The rain stopped, visibility cleared and German artillery and machine gun fire opened up on the isolated territorials. Rain recommenced but German shelling continued as 199th Brigade, including 2/5 (Wigan) Manchester Regiment moved forward and with the survivors of the original attack. attempted to hold the line against German counter attacks.

The scene was chaotic as the Manchesters desperately defended their section of the line. Their adjutant, Lieutenant Brown, regardless of enemy fire, moved constantly among his soldiers sheltering in the shell holes, encouraging and organising the men.

Lance-sergeant John Chantry repeatedly took out rations and ammunition to the front line and brought back wounded men. Private J.W. Sykes, a stretcher bearer crawled out under fire and successfully treated the survivors from a shell burst which had killed eleven men and wounded thirteen others. Corporal R.C. Hanson, the headquarters signaller, carried messages to all parts of the line after all other

signallers had been killed. Lance-corporal McLennox, the headquarters clerk, repeatedly brought in wounded men under shell fire. Another stretcher-bearer, Private John Dickinson, was buried by a shell, dug himself out and continued with his work. The line held, but only 500 yards had been gained at a cost of 3,000 casualties for the division.

66 DIVISION

	Killed	Wounded	Missing	Total
Officers	24	76	9	109
Other ranks	477	2,059	474	3,010
2/5Manchesters				
Officers	0	1	0	1
Other ranks	30	94	17	141

Of the missing Manchesters, only six men returned. At six in the evening, the division was relieved by the 43rd. Australian Brigade. When he arrived, the Australian commanding officer was aghast at what he found, writing later:-

> "The slope was littered with dead, theirs and ours. I got to one pill-box to find it a mass of dead so I passed to the one ahead. Here I found 50 men alive of the Manchesters. Never have I seen men so broken and demoralised. They were huddled up behind the pill-box in the last stages of exhaustion and fear. Fritz had been sniping at them all day and accounted for fifty seven. The dead and the dying lay in piles. The wounded were numerous, unattended and weak. Some had been there for four days."
> Australian Official History. p906-7.

For the first time, the new British tactics had failed. The task of capturing the whole distance in one day instead of pausing to consolidate had proved too much. The British Official History sums up what happened:-

> "The roads and tracks across the battle area had gravely deteriorated. Three months of persistent shelling and blocked water courses and the mass of shell holes frustrated every attempt to drain the water away. Up to 4th. October, there had been no serious difficulty (sic) but in certain areas conditions did become impassable. The entire valley of the Steenbeek was a porridge of mud. No progress could be made with the plank roads as the

planks either sank in the mire or floated away. Artillery guns sank up to their axles in mud, some up to their muzzles, Even when mounted on a gun platform, a foundation of road metal and reed fascines topped by a double level of beech wood slabs nailed together, which took two days to construct, many guns sank into the mud after a few rounds had been fired."

Most affected, of course, were the front line infantry who suffered in three main ways. Everyday living conditions were more primitive than prehistoric man had endured centuries before, no intricate sophisticated trench systems, no deep dugouts, no underground tunnels, instead the soldiers sheltered in water-filled craters without protection from the elements, exposed, cold, freezing, hungry, completely at the mercy of the enemy artillery, regularly shelled and gassed, worn out by lack of sleep, never knowing when their next meal would arrive.

It was impossible to advance to the attack in regulation order. Water-filled shell holes and pools of water on the surface had to be avoided so restricting the direction of the attack. Feet stuck in the clinging mud and the slow moving, stumbling infantry made easy targets. Rifles clogged with mud and became unusable, as did machine guns, Percussion shells failed to detonate on impact due to the soft ground which also absorbed the explosions of those that did.

The transport animals, horses and mules, suffered equally if not more so than their drivers. Many were hit and lay in the mud, uncomprehending the chaos around and since it was impossible for them to be moved, they had to be shot to put them out of their agony.

While the Germans too lived in appalling front-line conditions and had to counter attack over the same awful No-Man's-Land, the British alone had to struggle across a waste land of mud and water to bring up supplies to the front line. As they advanced, the British widened the 'mud belt' between the old front line of June, 1917 and the current one while the Germans could reach their forward troops across relatively undamaged terrain as they were slowly pushed back.

It was now that Haig's chief staff officer, Lieutenant General Sir Lawrence Kiggell, who had spent most of the war in the rear areas, visited the front line to see conditions for himself. According to legend[1] he broke down and cried after saying, *"Good God, did we send men to fight in this?"* His guide, a line officer and a veteran of the trenches replied, *"It's worse further on."*

[1]Owen. 'Tempestuous Journey, Lloyd George, His Life and Times.' p402.

There was not much *'further on'* to go. A patrol of the 66th. Division had actually entered Passchendaele. Their memorial is the divisional badge in the stained glass window of the rebuilt church, plus the coat of arms of every Lancashire town whose men fought there. Wigan is the third from the top on the left window.

CHAPTER SIX: PASSCHENDAELE.

First Passchendaele. 12th. October, 1917.

There was now an overwhelming case for abandoning the campaign. The most carefully prepared assault had got nowhere. Against the protests of both the politicians and his generals, Haig insisted that the offensive must continue only three days later. Rain continued and in spite of heroic endeavour by the gunners and the roadmakers it was impossible to move the artillery to its planned positions. The supply of planks ran out and the pack animals were unable to move. Those that did sank in the mud and drowned. A journey which normally took a hour took seventeen! Even if ammunition arrived, it was so coated with mud as to be unusable until cleaned. Runners with messages took seventy two hours to reach the rear and return (if they were lucky) to the front line. The entire area in front of Passchendaele was either water or mud. Stretchers which normally took two or four men at most to carry, now needed sixteen working in relays of four.

Passchendaele village was again the main objective. The New Zealanders attacked gallantly but their task was beyond human capacity. The mud, the unbroken wire, the machine guns, were too much and they gained no ground at all for the loss of 2,735 casualties, their only failure of the campaign. The Australians took most of their objectives but were pushed back to their start line. To the north, the supporting attack by the Guards Division did reach its final position, as it had in every attack of the campaign.

An onlooker described the conditions under which the troops attacked:-

> "Imagination cannot conceive of the scene, the slough, into which our men plunged with packs on their backs and faced fire a thousand times. The shell craters yesterday were full to overflowing with water and the beeks (streams) were thrown out of bounds by the great gunfire.
>
> Our artillery barrage moved forward at a slow, crawling pace but it could not easily be followed. It took men an hour and a half to cover 150 yards. Our barrage went on, the German barrage came down and from the enemy's blockhouses came the chattering of machine guns and in the great stretch of swamp, the men struggled."
>
> WO 10th. November, 1917.

German artillery counter attacked, first firing sneeze gas, which made it difficult to wear respirators, followed by mustard gas, which blistered the body and damaged the throat and eyes. Gunner Thomas Charles Jones, in the Royal Field Artillery, a 37 years old father of six, from Golborne, was gassed and later wrote home from a hospital bed in Leicester:-

> "My mouth and stomach burned like fire and for a week I was blind but my sight has now returned. It was just like someone throwing mustard into my face."
> LJ 16th. November, 1917.

Gunner Jones was only one of thousands in both front lines and rear positions who were disabled during this period. The attack was a costly failure.

Second Passchendaele 26th. October to 10th. November, 1917.

Even Haig agreed that conditions were now so bad that further attacks should be postponed until the roads could be repaired, the artillery moved forward and a more effective bombardment made possible. So followed a fortnight's pause during which all this was done but the weather was still not good, there were some fine, even sunny days but several with showers.

Just when he needed every available man, Haig then faced two unexpected demands on his resources. The French asked if the British could take over an extra section of front and knowing of the poor state of the French army, Haig reluctantly agreed. Shortly after, the Germans broke through the Italian front at Caporetto, advancing several miles and capturing 180,000 prisoners. Five divisions were sent from the Western Front to Italy, battle hardened troops Haig could ill-afford to lose. Nevertheless the offensive continued. Four Canadian divisions were transferred from near Arras where they had so magnificently captured Vimy Ridge earlier in the year.

Just before six in the morning on the 26th. October, 1917 the Third and Fourth Canadian Divisions attacked. The previous day had been fine and cool but at midnight, just as the assaulting brigades were forming up behind the jumping-off tapes, it began to rain yet again. On the right, the objective was only 400 yards distant and was taken, held through three counter attacks, lost to the fourth, retaken and held thereafter. On the left the attack halted halfway to the objective, 1,000 yards distant but for the first time, a position had been established on the higher, drier plateau west and south-west of Passchendaele.

On the Canadians' flanks, simultaneous attacks were made by British divisions to pin down the German reserves and to force the defenders to disperse their artillery fire. One of these was the 57th. Division another unit of West Lancashire Territorials:-

Brigade	**Battalion**	**Origin**
170th	2/5King's Own Royal Lancaster Regiment	Lancaster
	2/4Loyal North Lancashire Regiment	Preston
	2/5Loyal North Lancashire Regiment	Bolton
	4/5Loyal North Lancashire Regiment	Bolton
171st.	2/5King's Liverpool Regiment	Liverpool
	2/6King's Liverpool Regiment	Liverpool
	2/7King's Liverpool Regiment	Liverpool
	2/8King's Liverpool Regiment	Liverpool Irish
172nd.	2/9King's Liverpool Regiment	Liverpool
	2/10King's Liverpool Regiment	Liverpool Scottish
	2/4South Lancashire Regiment	Warrington
	2/5South Lancashire Regiment	St. Helens

The division had landed in France in February, 1917 and after limited experience in the trenches, this was to be its first attack. Once more the Official History recites the British division's experience, which must have been unimaginable, in calm understated language:-

> "From the onset, only very slow laborious progress could be made in mud so soggy that the men, knee deep, became stuck fast and easy targets for snipers. After superhuman efforts this most gallant attempt to achieve the impossible was abandoned."

Stumbling through the mud at the rate of less than a yard a minute, they were driven back to their starting positions. Casualties were enormous, with over eight thousand men killed, wounded and missing for not a yard of ground gained.

Tom Wall, a non-commissioned officer, who before the war, had been a reporter on the *'Wigan Observer'* took part in the attack on Passchendaele. His account of it is hair-raising:-

"We relieved (censored) on Sunday night and we were beat when we got there. Boche was very lively and we lost half a dozen N.C.O.'s and some men very early on. I got my section together and we made ourselves as comfortable as possible in a shell hole and stayed there all night and the next day and were informed that an attack would take place at 5.50 a.m. the next morning. We moved to where the line was, behind where the barrage would begin, in the early hours and during this time were shelled heavily and lost an officer who was very popular and who had gained the confidence of the whole company.

As the attack commenced, the Boche put a heavy barrage down at about the same time as we did. I was in the second wave. I lost the senior private in about a couple of minutes. He was knocked into a shell hole and drowned. I got one in the left arm, from a bullet and told the next man to carry on but when I found no bones were broken I ran after them and took charge again. This was the first open fighting we had been in and on my soul, the part where we were was really terrible. You sank up to you knees in mud and though your rifle was clean to begin with, it soon got clogged up with mud which got flung up with the shells as they burst.

We went on in single file when I got a bullet in the back and was hurled to the ground but fortunately not into a shell hole because I should surely have sunk with all the equipment and ammunition I was carrying. I could not walk but rolled into a hollow to escape the machine guns and huddled under the lip of the crater. From then on, the next nine or ten hours were the worst I have ever spent in my life or ever shall, I hope. Absolutely flat, like a rat in a trap, I lay on my stomach perfectly still while shells fell all around me and then, to put the tin hat on it, a couple of snipers discovered my whereabouts and let me have it. It was mighty wicked. The blighters must have known that I was wounded but they still kept pinking at me. Shells burst around me and although I expected to be blown to pieces every moment, my luck was in and none touched me.

As the surface of the ground changed, so did the level of the water and soon I was up to my waist. I decided to wait until nightfall and black my face and hands with mud, not that much would be required, and then crawl out on my stomach. To cap the lot, it rained and blew and then an aeroplane stared to fire. I thought the whole German army was after me. I got so fed up with it all that I was tempted to stand up and open my tunic and

let the sniper have a go. I was getting a bit strung up then and I'm glad I thought the better of it.
Shortly after five, I turned round and saw the back of the hole, incidentally, I don't think it would have been possible to find a 'Better 'Ole' (apologies to Bairnsfather) on that day, had been blown away. I saw a red cross flag fluttering on a recently captured pill-box, about fifty yards away. I spotted someone and he waved to come in. I got rid of my equipment and crawled through the opening in the crater so thoughtfully provided by a German shell and crawled along lying as low as possible.

A ______ (an adjective you can think of would not be strong enough) sniper kept potting at me the whole time but I kept low and reached safety. I was a wreck and I wonder how I didn't go off my head. One poor chap did because I could hear him singing in a shell hole but after a bit the firing silenced him. It was terrible. I went to look for the advanced dressing station and it took four hours floundering about in a sea of mud."
WO 10th. November, 1917.

On the 30th. October, the Third and Fourth Canadian Divisions pushed on and took the southern edge of Passchendaele village which they held against five counter attacks, completing the objective of their attack four days earlier. Five of the six assaulting battalions lost over fifty percent of their men and three Victoria Crosses were won.

The Canadians reshuffled their resources and on the 6th. November, 1917, a cold showery day, they took the ruins of Passchendaele. The First and Second Canadian divisions began their advance at 6 a.m. and in an hour the village was theirs. An hour later, they seized the crest beyond and the exhausted Germans declined to counter attack. On 10th November, the Canadians attacked again through a rain storm and within half an hour had pushed 500 yards beyond Passchendaele to the northern ridge and dug in overlooking the Flanders plain beyond. Victory was complete.

By this success and by their capture of Vimy Ridge and Hill 70 earlier in the year, the four Canadian corps proved themselves to be the finest soldiers on either side during the First World War. The equals of the Australians in fighting ability but with better discipline and control, the Canadians stand head and shoulders above the rest.

Surprisingly there were lots of local men among the Canadians. Many had emigrated in the years leading up to the war and on the outbreak of hostilities had volunteered for the armed forces of their new country. Private John Roberts aged 19 years, originally from Wigan had

lived in Canada for six years. Private Frank Cunliffe, aged 30 years, had also emigrated from Wigan years earlier as a young man, while Pioneer Robert Draper, formerly a fish dealer in Leigh before building a new life in the Dominions, was fifty nine! Private R. Moran, originally from St. Patrick Street and Private John Horrocks, were two other ex-Wiganers while Corporal Robert Hooton, whose parents still lived in Newtown, had emigrated to Canada as a young boy in 1912 and won the D.C.M. serving with a tunnelling company of the Canadian Royal Engineers. The Canadian Army archives must hold the names of many more.

The Canadians' success had been bought at a terrible price:-

	Officers			**Other ranks**			
	k	w	m	k	w	m	Total
26th.-30th. October							
3 Canadian	56	104	0	1174	2193	3	3530
4 Canadian	36	78	0	795	2044	9	2922
6th.-10th. November							
1 Canadian	43	70	0	577	1993	5	2688
2 Canadian	34	77	2	928	20	3	2954
Total	169	329	2	3474	1816	20	12,094

Wigan had already provided two full battalions of soldiers, the 1/5 and 2/5 Manchester Regiment, and now a third, the 3/5 Manchesters was amalgamated into a training unit with the 3/6 and 3/7 Battalions. In November, 1917, Wilfred Owen, recuperating from trench fever contracted on the Western Front during the Passchendaele offensive was posted to this new cadre at Scarborough. Here Owen wrote some of his best work, turning into poetry his experiences in the trenches, including one of his finest poems, 'Exposure'.

Once more he was destined not to fight in a local unit, for in September, 1918, he re-joined the 2nd. Manchesters in France just in time for the final advance to victory. He was killed in action on 4th. November, 1918, exactly one week before the Armistice.

CONCLUSIONS.

Passchendaele was a victory, a tragic victory, but there could be no denying it, nor the immense losses needed to bring it about, nor the conditions under which it was fought, both of which have since obscured the campaign's true strategic worth by dominating subsequent discussion of events.

Casualties were indeed heavy, more than the two earlier Ypres battles but lighter than Verdun and much less than the Somme:-

CASUALTIES

	British	French	German	Total
1st. Ypres (1914)	58,000	50,000	130,000	238,000
2nd (Ypres (1915)	60,000	10,000	35,000	105,000
Somme (1916)	420,000	195,000	437,000	1,052,000
Verdun (1916)		370,000	337,000	707,000
3rd. Ypres (1917)	338,000	9,000	260,000	601,000

Indeed they were far lighter than the battles to come in 1918:-

CASUALTIES

	British	German
1918 German Offensive	355,000	1,000,000
1918 Allied offensive	353,000	760,000[1]

Tactically the Passchendaele campaign brought immense advantages to the British Army. On reaching the crest of the low plateau ridge, a British officer looked back at his former positions:-

> "One felt amazed that the Boche had ever let anyone live in our trenches. We knew that we were overlooked but not to the extent we were, for thousands of yards into our rear positions."

What else did the terrible losses achieve? True, the campaign failed to break out into northern Belgium, an overoptimistic ambition in any case. True it failed to recapture the Belgian coast and get rid of the U-boat menace, again an optimistic objective which may well have been included in the list of aims for political as much as military reasons.

[1]Plus desertions and refusals to serve which could have been another 750,000 to 1,000,000.

There is no doubt that Haig's other aims were entirely successful. The Germans were drawn away from the French sector of the front and the French were not attacked again in 1917 so that after a delay of some months, the French Army was able to mount an offensive and on 24th. October, 1917, added to the pressure on Germany.

The casualty figures alone failed to tell the full story of the British Army's greatest achievement, the wearing down of the German Army, a process begun a year earlier on the Somme[1], a fact too easily recognised by the German high command:-

> "The sufferings, privations and exertions which the soldiers had to bear were inexpressible. The Hell of Verdun was exceeded by Flanders ....
> No division could last more than a fortnight in this hell. Then it had to be relieved by fresh troops ....
> The battle consumed the German strength to such a degree that the harm done could not be repaired."
> von Kuhl 'Der Weltkrieg 1914-18'.

Captured documents and prisoners testified to the effects of the campaign on German morale, both at the front and at home as is shown in these extracts from some soldiers' letters:-

> "We had colossal losses. The company was originally 140 strong and on 12th. August when we paraded we were only 18 men."

> "If this goes on and we go up to the front line tomorrow, I shall fall out and not go up again."

> "There is as little prospect of my coming out of this alive as there is of a victorious peace for our country and that is the general opinion among the men."

And in a letter from home found in a dead soldier's pocket:-

> "Hundreds of people stand in front of the butchers, cheesemongers and egg shops. Each person gets one egg a week sometimes none at all. We don't get sugar any longer. There is nothing not even when one has money. It is high time the war ended."

[1]See companion volume, 'The Finest of All'. Local Men on the Somme.

A contributory factor to the British soldiers' mental domination of their adversaries was the way in which they had overcome the new German defensive tactics. Since the Somme, the Germans had only held their front trenches with the minimum force required, so reducing losses through artillery bombardment and relied on immediate counterattacks. When these hastily organised counter attacks failed, they changed to more carefully planned attacks the next day. When these failed, they reverted to a more strongly-held front line but this only resulted in heavier casualties. The German High Command realised that they could never win the war by remaining on the defensive and that their only chance was to attack. They did so in March, 1918 but without ensuring the resources to bring about victory. Their offensive failed and before the year was out, the war was over.

Accompanying the decline in German morale, there was, at first a corresponding rise in that of the British soldier. Many, such as Private H.W. Hunt, were resigned to a continuing long, hard slog to victory but they never doubted the final outcome:-

> "All we know is that we keep plodding on with the task of wearing down the Germans and we are looking forward to the day when the detestable Hun will get the knockout blow. The war must go on until the savage Hun beasts are tamed."
> WE 1st. September, 1917.

And another soldier:-

> "The superior personal qualities of our troops and the leading of our officers have found scope long hitherto denied to them. It is a tremendous and even glorious fact that our new armies, the civilians of yesterday, have found themselves capable of mastering the best soldiers of the Prussian military tradition. The Germans are being constantly exposed to relentless and successful attacks by enemies their equal in discipline and superiors in numbers and munitions. There is no doubt that the morale of the German army has been affected. It is evidenced by the way large bodies of Germans have offered themselves as prisoners in recent actions.
> WO 1st. September, 1917.

Yet the prolonging of the campaign into October and November only served to undermine British morale. Crown Prince Rupprecht of

Bavaria hitherto very impressed by the bearing and demeanour of British prisoners noted that they were now sullen, resentful and critical of their officers. Even the British Official History admitted the campaign's influence on the British fighting men:-

> "The discomfort of living conditions in the forward areas and the strain of fighting with indifferent success had discouraged all ranks more than any other operation fought during the war so that discontent was general."
> Official History 1917 Vol.2, p209.

Another misconception of the Passchendaele campaign is that the British High Command particularly Commander-in-Chief Sir Douglas Haig, were ignorant of the front-line situation. True, as was the custom at that time Haig himself never visited the battle area, but he was kept regularly informed of conditions by his liaison officers, by the artillery and engineer officers, and by his own staff officers, who inspected the battlefield and whose reports did not minimise the dreadful conditions. One staff officer remembered later:-

> "I went up and spent some hours at brigade and battalion head quarters. I could see and heard much about the awful conditions. On my return, I dictated and signed what could only be described as a violent report. After dinner, I was sent for and taken to the C-in-C's room. There was nobody else there. Sir Douglas took me across to a big wall map and told me to elaborate on my report. I did this at considerable length and with great emphasis. Although very attentive Haig made little or no comment. At the end he said, "Thank you, Major Osborne. Goodnight."
> Letter in the 'Spectator', 10th January, 1958.

There was no blind ignorance. They knew. Even the civilians back home knew. Early in 1917, a delegation of Lancashire coal mining trade unionists including the future Wigan M.P., Harry Twist, visited the front. Their report says it all.

> "A more complete destruction of a once-peaceful countryside could not be imagined. The whole ground for miles is ploughed up many feet deep by shell fire which the rain has turned into a quagmire."

The delegation crossed on duckboards to the British trenches ending up 300 yards from the German lines and obtained a comprehensive view of conditions. They saw everything. It is difficult to accept that the High Command was ignorant of the facts when the civilians knew. It had always been recognised that conditions in Flanders were more difficult than on the higher ground further south in France. Scores of letters from the front during the early years of the war testified to the awful conditions. Corporal Hampson, 71 Battery Royal Field Artillery wrote to Upper St. Stephen Street, Wigan:-

> "We are having rotten weather here. It is raining every day and we are up to our knees in mud and we are better off than the infantry in the trenches."
> WE 14th. January, 1915.

Another Wiganer, Private Dyke in the Lancashire Fusiliers, wrote:-

> "All the time we are waist deep in clay and water. I had to go to the rear with eleven others to draw company rations. We had to go for one and half miles down a trench which communicates with the firing line trench. We were up to our chins in water and when we got back, the food floated away."
> WE 30th. January, 1915.

Four days later, they were relieved:-

> "I could not get out of the trench because I was stuck in the mud, in fact I was nearly buried, only my face was showing. They got me out by cutting my equipment and putting ropes under my arms and pulling me out."

Descriptions of the conditions under which the campaign was fought tower above all political and strategical wrangling. A Canadian soldier wrote to a friend in Crooke:-

> "To describe the ground over which the boys have to go is pretty hard but it is damnable hard work to overcome the obstacles that are in front of them. The battle has been fought in a wilderness of craters and shell holes."
> WO 1st. September, 1917.

Private William Carrington, originally from Park Road, Wigan and serving with the Australians, was wounded in the Battle of Menin Road, and wrote home from his hospital bed describing that and later attacks:-

> "Only those who have gone over those grim, ghastly, torn and shattered battlefields of Ypres and lived with death in its entirety can feel the true depth of admiration for the terrible and cruel hardships they had to surmount to take their objective. Tired, worn, hungry, wet to the skin, with clogged rifles and guns, they gained what they set out to do. God's very presence must have been with them. The physical pain from fatigue, must have been acute for we Australians know what it is like to plod on knee deep in mud and mire."
> WE 17th. October, 1917.

> "Nothing I can write will remotely convey the look of such ground and the horror of it. Unless one has seen such vast fields of barren earth, blasted for miles by shellfire, pitted by deep craters so close that they look like holes in a sieve and so deep that the tallest man can drown in them when they are filled with water. They were not ponds and pits but great deep lakes, in which the bitter corruption of the battlefield floated. Our men had to haul one leg after the other out of the deep, sucking bog and could hardly do that. And lots of them were held up in the bog as in glue and sank up to their waists."
> WO 6th. November, 1917.

Tom Wall vividly described the conditions under which he himself had fought:-

> "You will have read of the conditions up there at the front so I shan't need to describe them but it is really frightful, a swamp for miles, mud, and such mud, and shell holes filled with water. To get to your lines you have three miles I should say, along duckboards then along muddy paths and then you have shell holes to convert into places where you 'reside' for a couple of days or so."
> WO 6th. November, 1917.

Yet it would be a mistake to think that the entire campaign was fought under these conditions. The first three weeks in September were

mostly sunny with a drying wind and the taking of all objectives with unprecedented ease tells its own story. It was the cumulative effects of the earlier wet weather and three months persistent shelling followed by the onset of a wet autumn which caused further deterioration of battlefield conditions:-

> "Since early in October, mud had become a factor of the greatest importance. Even August had been unusually wet and since then the ground, always water-logged and now thoroughly cut up, had steadily got worse. The mere movement of artillery and ammunition was a Herculean task. It was scarcely possible to walk off the duckboards. Mules were constantly engulfed and guns in considerable numbers were swallowed up in the sea of mud."
> Rawlins, 'British Artillery in France, 1914 to 1918'.

The controversy over Passchendaele should not be whether or not the battles should ever have been started, Messines was at the start of the summer, but given the delays, whether it should have been prematurely concluded at the end of September. Although near the coast, Flanders in summer, comes under continental climatic influences where prolonged high pressure brings hot, dry weather, frequently including short heavy thunderstorms, seldom long lasting but leaving the ground sodden for long periods. Then as summer ends, maritime influences take over where depressions moving in from the sea bring prolonged periods of rain. Once October arrived, conditions were never going to improve. After the abject failure at Poelcappelle on 9th. October, the campaign should have been stopped.

This is borne out by analysis of the causality figures The entire campaign saw about 245,000 British and Empire soldiers killed, wounded, missing or prisoners. Of these, some 139,000 men or 57% were in the 65 days up to 4th. October while 106,000 or 43% were for the following 34 days until 10th. November.

And the survivors? All expected to return home as heroes. History shows that this was not the case and early in the war a perceptive Wigan soldier voiced his concerns in a letter home:-

> "Will the British public ever be able to understand half the sufferings our brave fellows have endured to enable us at home to go about out duties in safety and what will be our attitude towards them at the end of the war?"
> WO 1st. January, 1916.

The last word on Passchendaele must go to one who fought there, Lieutenant Colonel Graham Hutchinson, D.S.O., M.C. of the Machine Gun Corps:-

> ".... men heavy eyed, yet who slept little and intermittently, eyes seared with blood, dim and discoloured with mustard gas, unshaven, haggard, grey-faced, grimy, clothing encrusted with drying yellow mud. Men lived unbelievably on the outer crust of a honeycomb, its honey being putrid water. Each death pool was separated from the next by a foot of mud. Stuck to the pool's greasy slithering side, huddled above the stinking water, men lived out their days and nights swept by shell and machine gun fire and soaked by gas.
> Passchendaele remains a monument to British tenacity and courage and at the same time a sheer waste of life and wholly destructive of morale. The scene beggars description. Wounded men lost in the trackless undulations, cried bitterly, day and night from the shell holes into which they had fallen, until death stifled their cries as they subsided into the slime or were drowned in the stagnant water holes. There were scarcely ten square yards of ground or water where there did not protrude an arm, a leg or a helmeted head, some German but mostly British. History must write of Passchendaele that it remains a military crime. No possible excuse, no extenuating circumstances, political, strategical, tactical, exists for its futilities."

Unfortunately the longest lasting legacy of Passchendaele was that it fixed in peoples' minds the belief that war was futile and should be avoided at all costs. It gave support and encouragement to those in the pacifist movement, those who believed in appeasement and those who wanted peace at any price. In so doing, it held back British rearmament during the twenties and thirties and as a result it condemned a subsequent generation to military unpreparedness and unnecessary losses at the start of the next war. This incorrect interpretation of Passchendaele ensured that those who laid down their lives did so in vain. Lost lives. Lost but not forgotten.

PHOTOGRAPHS

Photograph 1. (Page 5)
The ground is covered with the bodies of fallen British soldiers in a photograph taken early in the war. In the background, two soldiers struggle through a very primitive barbed wire entanglement.

Photograph 2. (Page 11)
Twin shell bursts throw up soil, smoke and metal fragments.

Photograph 3. (Page 13)
The indented shape of the trenches can be clearly seen in these preserved positions on top of Vimy Ridge where the concrete 'sandbags' create a sanitised version.

Photograph 4. (Page 15)
Today, this preserved trench in Sanctuary Wood has a mud floor several inches deep, even in summer.

Photograph 5. (Page 17)
An example of how near the opposing trenches often were. These on top of Vimy Ridge, preserved for posterity in concrete, are only twenty yards apart. Sometimes they were a mile distant but averaged 400 yards.

Photograph 6. (Page 19)
A German pillbox at the east end of Tyne Cot CWGC cemetery, next to some of the 12,000 graves.

Photograph 7. (Page 35)
A young-looking German prisoner is searched. Notice he is wearing spectacles.

Photograph 8. (Page 37)
It is very difficult to photograph a mine crater at ground level. This one is on top of Vimy Ridge is less than ten percent of the size of the Messines craters.

Photograph 9. (Page 39)
Another photograph taken early in the war shows medics treating the wounded among the dead

Photograph 10. (Page 55)
A sinister-looking German pillbox in Langemarcke German Military Cemetery. Notice the different type of headstone and instead of individual inhumations there were collective ones to commemorate comradeship. Altogether 44,000 Germans are buried here, 24.000 in one mass grave.

Photograph 11. (Page 71)
Mud was bad enough but when oil spillage added to soldiers' difficulties they must have despaired.

Photograph 12. (Page 75)
Three German pillboxes on the road between Ypres and Armentieres must have been an awesome strong point.

Photograph 13. (Page 79)
This large well-lit, airy dugout in the chalk rock south of the Ypres sector was in stark contrast to the degrading living conditions of the Ypres salient.

Photograph 14. (Page 80)
Even these well preserved shell holes fail to give the complete picture of the intensity of shelling in the Ypres salient.

Photograph 15. (Page 83)
A rural idyll utterly devastated. A scene repeated countless time on the Western Front.

Photograph 16 (Page 86)
Two guns of a British battery destroyed in transit by accurate German artillery fire.

Photograph 17. (Page 88)
A British soldier, wounded in the leg, receives a drink from a comrade's water bottle.

Photograph 18. (Page 91)
Another view of the destroyed battery shown in the earlier photograph. The fate of horses on the Western Front was pitiful.

Photograph 19. (Page 93)
A more realistic but still far from accurate section of former trenches in Sanctuary Wood just south of Ypres.

Photograph 20. (Page 95)
The restored Menin Gate. Rebuilt after the war to far greater grandeur than before. The gate's panels carry the names of over 53,000 soldiers who marched through its predecessor to fight in the Ypres Salient and have no known grave. The stone panels at Tyne Cot CWGC cemetery carry the names of 34,000 more.